About the author

Chris Nothdurfter has been producing for ten years. He has worked with bands as well as on his own projects. As a songwriter he has produced demos for a wide range of genres spanning from German *"Schlager"* Pop music to blazing Death Metal. While his first musical influences were classic Heavy Metal bands such as Metallica and Iron Maiden he nowadays enjoys most band-oriented music out there (as long as it's crafted well). Chris is also involved in Live/Tour Production as well as a number of non music-related projects in the fields of Film & Video, Health, Fitness & Nutrition, Entrepreneurship, and Marketing.

This page intentionally left blank

#HitIt

The Ultimate Guide to Programming Drums

Chris Nothdurfter

Copyright © 2014 by Christoph Nothdurfter

Published by Christoph Nothdurfter

ISBN-13: 978-1506010472

ISBN-10: 1506010474

All rights reserved. No part of this publication may be reproduced, stored in a retrieval system, or transmitted, in any form or by any means, electronic, mechanical, photocopying, recording, or otherwise, without the prior written permission of the publisher.

All screenshots and illustrations by Christoph Nothdurfter except drum kit illustration by Ofirka991 at the Hebrew Wikipedia project.

Edited by James Bogdanis.

Cover concept by Christoph Nothdurfter. Cover photo and artwork by Bobby Kostadinov (www.soundlurkerstudio.com).

Acknowledgements

This book would have never been written if it weren't for **Jan Pannenbäcker** who encouraged me to work on my own projects. Thank you for always providing valuable feedback on all my crazy ideas and for the endless amount of inspiring conversations.

Thanks to **James Bogdanis** for taking the time to edit and proofread this book. Because of you, the people reading this book might actually understand what I was trying to say. I'll repay you with an endless amount of random Snapchats. Thanks buddy, I really appreciate it.

Special thanks to **Bobby Kostadinov** who not only did an amazing job with the cover of this book but has also proven to be a reliable collaborator on a number of projects over the last couple of years. We have worked together on entire albums yet we have never met in person. Can you believe it?

Last but not least I'd like to thank all my friends whom I've neglected a great deal during the writing process of this book. I often let my projects consume me fully. I'm working on that. Thank you for your patience.

Contents

ABOUT THE AUTHOR 1

ACKNOWLEDGEMENTS 5

FOREWORD 11

How to use this book 12

THE BASICS 15

The Pieces of a drum kit 15

MIDI Basics 19

MIDI Mapping 21

Beat Basics 25

Four to the floor 27

A drummer is not an Octopus 31

POP 33

Building the beat 34

Hi-hat barking 39

Tom beats 41

Sidestick 45

Half-time feel 47

The Ride cymbal 48

Bass drum variations 48

Pop fills 50

Crash cymbals and final tips 57

ROCK 59

Snare drum Comping 61

Ghost notes 63

The Ride cymbal 65

Advanced fills 65

Triplet fills 72

Ending fills 74

METAL 77

Locking-in with palm muting 77

Double Bass drum beats 79

Blast beats 86

Basic Metal fills 94

Advanced Metal fills 103

Accompanying element variations 108

The Crash cymbals 109

HUMANIZING BEATS 111

Quantization 112

Velocities 115

    Ghost notes 120

    Hi-hat 121

    Cymbals 124

    Crescendos 125

    Double Bass drum beats 128

    Blast beats 129

    Fine-tuning velocities 130

BONUS CHAPTER: ODD TIME SIGNATURES 133
- 6/8 time 133
- 5/4 time 137
- 7/4 time 140

BONUS CHAPTER: MIXING TIPS 145
- Different types of Drum Software and Routing 146
- Cymbals 147
- Bass drum 148
- Snare drum 148
- Toms 149
- Room sound and Reverb 150
- Parallel compression 151
- Sample replacement 152

FINAL WORDS 153

Foreword

It was early fall 2004. I had just bought my first multi-effects guitar pedal and had chosen a specific model that doubled as a USB audio interface. Like most aspiring rock stars, I wanted to finally record my masterpieces and I was going to do it all by myself. So, I bought a cable from eBay that allowed me to hook up my interface to my home stereo (I had never heard of studio monitors back then) and I was good to go. I'd be the guitar player, the bass player, the songwriter, the engineer, the producer and the mixer of my very first demo. However, there was one problem. I needed a drummer as well. *"Screw it"*, I said to myself, *"I'm going to be the drummer as well."*. And this is how it all started.

At the time I had been tabbing out my all my songs using Guitar Pro for a while and I came up with drum parts to go along with my riffs. However, I had no way of combining actual recorded guitar tracks with the drum parts. So I found a seemingly clever work-around: Guitar Pro was capable of exporting audio tracks! It sounded horrible for all the guitar parts, but the drums were somewhat usable (and so was the bass). So, what I did was program just one hit of each drum and cymbal, then exported to individual audio clips. One by one I created my first "sample library". My audio interface came with a free copy of the worst DAW (digital audio workstation or recording software) ever, which I gladly used to record my guitar parts. Since it had no MIDI capabilities, I imported the aforementioned samples and placed them wherever I needed them to be, in order to create the finished drum track. One. Hit. At. A. Time.

As you can imagine, this was a pretty tedious task and as I evolved as a songwriter I also kept exploring software that I could use to become a better producer. As years went by, better drum samples and software instruments came around. Using them continuously also improved my technique significantly, and now I'm here sharing with you what I have learned. By reading this book, you will learn how to write and program your own drum tracks from scratch. In the process, we will cover everything you'll need to know in order to create drums that sound convincing, without ever being in the same room with an actual drummer. Sound tempting? Well then, follow me.

How to use this book

If you already have a good understanding of how your drum software works and how to get a little beat off the ground, you can skip the first chapter and go straight to the genre-specific sections that interest you the most. However, keep in mind that some techniques and principles can be applied to more than one genre. For example, you might be able to use something from the Pop chapter in your Rock songs. So if you have the time, it definitely pays to at least skim over every chapter briefly. I've kept the chapter on humanization separate, as it might very well be the most important one. Be sure to take an in-depth look at it, if you are really serious about making your drums sound as natural as possible. Last but not least there are two *bonus* chapters. I initially didn't plan on covering odd time signatures and mixing drums respectively, but a lot of people requested it, so I decided to include it after all.

You can download a MIDI file containing the examples from this book at www.drumprogrammingguide.com/midi. Make sure to apply the laid out principles yourself for the best learning experience.

I really hope that you enjoy the book and that you will learn a lot from it. Please make sure to join the Facebook User group "**#HitIt – The Ultimate Drum programming Group**" to connect with other producers and ask any questions you might have. I look forward to lively discussion and to learn from you as well.

Direct link: www.drumprogrammingguide.com/facebook-group

As a reader of this book you are also more than welcome to join my e-mail list. You'll get access to exclusive content and opportunities that are for my readers only. In the past we've already had a contest in cooperation with Toontrack where readers could enter to win copies of EZdrummer 2. You'll also be able to contact me directly with any questions you might have.

E-mails will be infrequent and I promise not to fill up your inbox. Needless to say I don't send spam and I will never give away your e-mail address. It'll be possible for you to immediately unsubscribe from the list at any time if you should wish to do so at some point in the future.

Go to the following website to sign up for free:
www.drumprogrammingguide.com/readers-newsletter

The Basics

In this section I will go over a few essential basics that we need to establish in order to be able to program the grooves that'll make us all rock out on that set of air drums. First thing's first.

The Pieces of a drum kit

I consciously noticed drums for the first time when I was a little kid, and watched a marching band play. I remember being fascinated by the pounding rhythm they had going on. What kept them playing in time and marching at the same time were what people called "the big drum" and "the small drum" as well as clash cymbals. Years later when I came in contact with all sorts of heavy music, most drummers I met couldn't make a lot of the names for these instruments I had inherited from the town folks. Things were named differently in the world out there and more importantly there was actually a lot more to a drum kit than just a small and a big drum and a pair of cymbals. So, if you've never played drums yourself or talked about drums with other musicians, you might not be familiar with the individual pieces of a drum kit either. In this case, read on to find out what they are called and their purpose in modern music. If you already know about different shells and cymbals you can skip this section.

Figure 1: The pieces of a drum kit

The Bass drum (marked 1 in the diagram): This drum is sometimes also referred to as the Kick drum. Both names are often used interchangeably. In order to hit the Bass drum, the drummer uses his right foot to step on a pedal that moves a beater that in turn hits the drum. It produces a deep and punchy sound. This is what moves your pants at live shows. Together with the Snare drum (see below), the Bass drum forms the foundation of a vast majority of beats. While Pop and Rock music mostly use one Bass drum, in Metal, two Bass drums are very common. Metal drummers alternate between two Bass drums using both feet. Therefore, they are able to produce more Bass drum beats very quickly. They might also just use one actual Bass drum in conjunction with a special pedal that allows them to hit the same drum with both their feet.

The Snare drum (3): Next to the Bass drum, the Snare drum is the second constant in today's drum beats. Most of the time, a right-handed drummer will play it with his left hand. In contrast to all other drums on a standard drum set, the Snare drum usually has rattles (the actual "snares") of gut, metal wire, or similar material stretched across it's bottom head, which provides its distinctive loud and punchy sound. Some drummers keep an additional Snare drum around their kit (sometimes called an Auxiliary or Aux Snare) for a specific sound or certain songs. It's not uncommon for an Aux Snare to produce a significantly higher, louder, and/or punchier sound than the main Snare, since they are used as a special effect.

The Hi-hat (5): The Hi-hat is probably the most important cymbal in modern music. Together with a Bass and Snare drum, it forms the most basic of drum sets. It is the main rhythm driver, meaning that it is usually being hit in a constant manner in order to give the rest of the band something to listen out for so they can stay on the beat. In contrast to all other cymbals (see below), the drummer can either hit it with his sticks or use the Hi-hat pedal to play it as well. When he's not using the pedal to play it, he will usually cross his right hand over his left hand and hit it with a stick. The Hi-hat can be played open (when the corresponding pedal is released) or closed (with the drummers foot pushing down the pedal). If you are just looking for something constant and distinct, the closed position is the way to go. Open up the Hi-hat for a heavier feel. It's also possible to open and close the Hi-hat continuously using just the foot pedal. This way it sounds a little less pointy in comparison to when it's played with a stick, but it also frees up one of the drummer's hands that can in turn be used to possibly hit a Tom together with the Snare, as an example.

The Tom-Toms (2, 4): When talking about Tom-Toms, everybody just uses the term Toms so we'll refer to them like that from now on. The Toms are sort of similar to the Bass drum, but they are smaller and hit with a drumstick instead of a pedal. They are mostly used for drum fills to connect two beats. In some cases they are also used to drive a rhythm pattern themselves. The bigger a Tom, the lower it's pitch will be. The bigger ones are usually situated on the floor on their own. These are known as Floor Toms, while the smaller ones are mounted on top of the Bass drum and are called Rack Toms (or Hi(gh) Toms). Right-handed drummers set them up left to right with the smallest Rack Tom on the left above the Bass drum, the Snare drum next to the Hi-hat and the biggest Floor Tom all the way on the right.

Crash cymbal(s) (6): Most Pop, Rock, and Metal drummers will have at least two of these on their drum kit. Their name sort of describes their sound, which is a somewhat harsh, when hit accordingly. Usually crashes have quite a lot of *attack*, meaning that the individual cymbal sound characteristics unfold rather quickly. In Pop and Rock, Crashes are mostly used to accentuate a new section of the song, while in Metal, they are sometimes also used to drive the song instead of the Hi-hat.

Ride cymbal (7): The Ride cymbal is used as an alternative to the Hi-hat. It's sound is somewhat similar to that of a Crash cymbal but due to it's larger size it has less attack. Rather than a crash sound, it produces a "ping" of sorts. The little part around the mounting point of the cymbal stand is called the Bell, and when hit it produces a different and even more outstanding sound than the rest of the cymbal. If hit really hard on the edge, it can also double as an alternative to Crash cymbals.

Splash cymbal, China cymbal (8, 9): These two types of cymbals are not necessarily found on every drummer's kit. Like the Crashes, they are used to put accents on certain beats. The Splash is kind of small and therefore produces a short "Splash" (duh!). A China cymbal's sound on the other hand is very distinct, sounding somewhat tinny with lots of attack.

Most drum kits you'll come across will probably consist of
- one Bass drum (maybe with a Double Bass drum pedal),
- one Snare drum,

- one Hi-hat,
- three Toms (two Rack Toms and one Floor Tom)
- one Ride and
- two Crashes.

In order to be useful for the biggest possible amount of people using the vast array of different drum software out there, I'll focus the beats explained in this book around these drum kit elements. Don't be surprised if your particular drum software offers a multitude of further options.

Now that we know what all the different parts of a drum kit are called, we need to figure out how to make our computer play them. In order to achieve this we use the latest cutting-edge technology from 1982, the so-called Musical Instrument Digital Interface protocol, or MIDI for short.

MIDI Basics

I wish I was joking at the end of the last section but I wasn't. MIDI dates back to the early 1980s and is still used today. Now, shouldn't it be outdated you ask? Yes, by today's computer technology standards it should be. But then again: "If it ain't broke don't fix it."

I remember my first encounter with MIDI sometime in the Mid-90s. I was a kid and I got an Entertainer Keyboard as my second musical instrument, right after I had mastered the Recorder with two years of hard work. Between learning to play masterpieces like Michael Holm's "Mendocino", Al Martino's "Spanish Eyes" and Kenny Rogers' "Lucille", I noticed my Keyboard had two plugs next to the power input that I had never used before. They were mysteriously labeled "MIDI In" and "MIDI out". At the time no one could explain to me what it was used for, and the Internet was very much in its infancy. So, I was left curious for another couple of years until I finally found like-minded people that knew somebody who had told them a story or two about what MIDI could do. What I found out though, was that I needed a MIDI interface for my computer in order to be able to use my keyboard's magical MIDI abilities. It wasn't until yet a few years later that I finally got one with my first real audio interface. Now I could use all the Synthesizer Plug-ins I had on my computer without having to literally draw in all the notes I wanted it to play. Instead, I could use my good old Entertainer Keyboard to do that now. Good times.

Fast-forward ten years. What can you learn from this? MIDI is a way to tell any instrument that's capable of receiving MIDI input data which notes to play for how long and how loud to play them. That's really all we need to know for our purpose. Regardless of whatever DAW you are using, the basic setup process for drum programming is as follows:

1. Add a MIDI track to your project.

2. Set the newly created MIDI track's output to the drum software of your choice. (Depending on your Recording Software's workflow, you might have to load an instance of the drum software first.)

3. Create a MIDI event on your project's timeline and open up your Recording Software's MIDI editor (Usually double-clicking on the event does the trick.).

4. Start filling up that MIDI event with grooves.

5. Rock out.

With this book I will help you become an expert at #4. For the other tasks please refer to the manuals of your DAW and your drum software respectively. Don't worry; it's not going to take you more than five minutes to figure it out and maybe 10 seconds to actually do it.

If you've successfully checked off all the above you're probably eager to get going. In order to get the groove on we need to figure out how to tell our drum software which drums to play when and how loud it should play them. In other words, we need to create MIDI notes that correspond to our desired groove. How do we do that? If you've created a MIDI event and opened your DAW's MIDI editor, your screen should now mainly consist of a Piano roll (usually on the left side of the screen but that depends on your DAW) and a grid. The latter is where we'll build our grooves. For a simple test run, click a few keys on the Piano roll randomly. If you are hearing drum sounds then you are good to go. If you don't hear any sounds at all, make sure no channels are accidently muted in your project. If that didn't help, go back to the previous paragraph and make sure you've gone through all the necessary steps accordingly.

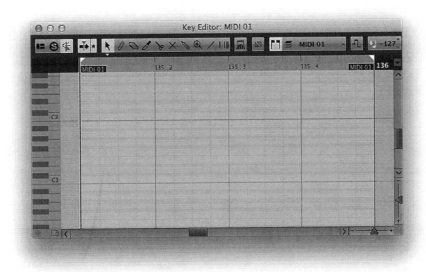

Figure 2: A MIDI editor window (Piano roll on the left and the grid on the center of the screen)

MIDI Mapping

Going through setup and testing in the last section you probably already realized there's a big problem: "How am I supposed to know which notes on the piano roll will produce which drum sounds?"

Old-school drum machines (like the ones on your favorite Vanilla Ice record) worked in a similar fashion, much in the same way as modern drum software does: The producer told the machine which sounds to play when and how loud to play them. At the time, a MIDI keyboard or a different input device might have been used, just like you used the Piano roll in your Recording Software a few seconds ago. Understandably, musicians and producers alike, then and now, don't want to test out which notes will produce which sounds on any given drum computer all the time. Luckily someone came up with General MIDI, or GM mapping for short. GM mapping is basically a guideline that standardizes which notes correspond to which sounds. Here it is for your reference:

MIDI note	Drum sound	MIDI note	Drum sound
B0	Acoustic Bass drum	B2	Ride Cymbal 2
C1	Electric Bass drum	C3	Hi Bongo
C#1	Side Stick	C#3	Low Bongo
D1	Acoustic Snare	D3	Mute Hi Conga
D#1	Hand clap	D#3	Open Hi Conga
E1	Electric Snare	E3	Low Conga
F1	Low Floor Tom	F3	High Timbale
F#1	Closed Hi-hat	F#3	Low Timbale
G1	High Floor Tom	G3	High Agogo
G#1	Pedal Hi-hat	G#3	Low Agogo
A1	Low Tom	A3	Cabasa
A#1	Open Hi-hat	A#3	Maracas
B1	Low-Mid Tom	B3	Short Whistle
C2	Hi-Mid Tom	C4	Long Whistle
C#2	Crash Cymbal 1	C#4	Short Guiro
D2	High Tom	D4	Long Guiro
D#2	Ride Cymbal	D#4	Claves
E2	Chinese Cymbal	E4	Hi Wood Block
F2	Ride Bell	F4	Low Wood Block
F#2	Tambourine	F#4	Mute Cuica
G2	Splash Cymbal	G4	Open Cuica
G#2	Cowbell	G#4	Mute Triangle
A2	Crash Cymbal 2	A4	Open Triangle
A#2	Vibraslap		

Figure 3: GM map

So, in a nutshell, any drum machine (software or hardware) that's mapped to GM will produce the drum sounds as shown above if you hit the corresponding MIDI notes on it. You may have noticed that there are a lot of percussion sounds and even some sound effects on the list. This is where it get's tricky. Modern music doesn't always have a whole lot of use for these, so current drum software doesn't necessarily include all of these samples. Instead, free MIDI notes are often used as aliases for sounds that the software includes. So for example you might find an open Hi-hat sound on A#1 (just like on the GM map) as well as on C3 (where the Hi Bongo used to be). Most drum software is laid out roughly according to the GM map so you can find the most important parts quickly. However, since different programs include a different level of sampling detail, it sometimes makes sense to group certain instruments on the mapping. For example, you might find all available Hi-hat sounds (Closed, different opening degrees, fully open, pedal, etc.) on consecutive notes on the piano roll for additional convenience.

In order to make it easy for you to find all the available drum sounds of any given piece of software, most manufacturers include a drum map or layout or a MIDI map or layout (descriptions vary) in their documentation. Go find that right now, because you're going to need it. If your DAW's MIDI capabilities are somewhat advanced, you might even be able to create a custom drum map that allows you to actually show the note descriptions (e.g. "Snare Head", "Snare Rimshot", "Hi-hat open", "Hi-hat closed", etc.) in addition to or instead of the MIDI notes in your DAW's MIDI editor to make programming even easier. Some DAWs might even allow you to visually re-arrange the available notes on the screen while leaving the actual MIDI notes in the background untouched to further optimize your workflow. Make sure to check your DAW's documentation to find out if it's capable to do that. If it isn't don't despair. Printing out the layout or mapping page of your drum software's documentation and putting it right in front of you on your desk will work just as good and you'll remember the most important notes in no time. In this book I will use no references to actual MIDI notes since everybody has their favorite drum software, and like I said, mapping differs. Luckily my DAW supports naming and re-arranging features and since they help keep things clear, I will use them in this book.

The following example is a simple beat consisting of a Bass drum, a Snare, and an open Hi-hat. In my case the actual MIDI notes behind that would be C1 for the Bass drum, D1 for the Snare drum and A#1 for the open Hi-hat. That just so happens to follow the GM mapping as well. As mentioned earlier you don't see that in the screenshot and you don't need to anyway. In order to program the beats, I will describe in this book just find the corresponding MIDI notes for your drum software as mentioned above, and use the rest of the given information accordingly.

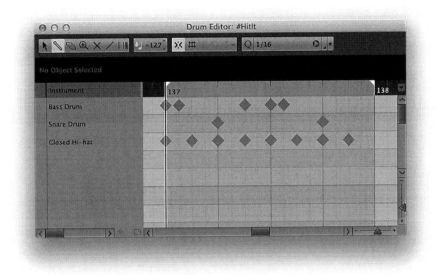

Figure 4: Simple beat example

Beat Basics

Ok, so we've successfully set everything up so we can start banging away on those virtual drums. To get the groove kicking, we still need to establish a few more fundamentals though. Besides all the technical formalities we also need to know about the musical aspects of modern Pop, Rock, and Metal music. Actually this even gets a little mathematical. Don't sweat it though, as long as you can count to four you're good because the majority of modern music is based on what's called a 4/4 groove. What this means, is that you can fit four 1/4 ("Quarter") notes in one measure (or bar, whichever you prefer). There are a lot of new terms so let's go over all of them.

Measure or bar: A measure is a segment of time in a piece of music. In sheet music measures are separated from each other with vertical lines. The main idea is to make reading sheet music easier, but there is also some use for measures in music production. Usually DAWs follow a grid and a timeline that allows you to keep track of where you are in the song or arrangement. Normally this can be set to either time or measures. Let's say your first Chorus clocks in at 32 seconds or after 16 measures and there's something you need someone else to fix. It's much more common (and easier) to just tell them the number of the measure than the actual time code. For now let's just make sure your DAW's timeline and/or grid is set to measures or bars, whatever they may be called. Please refer the manual to find out how to set it up.

1/4 notes and note values in general: The note value determines how long a certain note is played. If a beat contains just 1/4 notes this means we can fit four successive 1/4 notes in one measure, if it is set in 4/4 time. Got it? Now, if we include 1/16 ("Sixteenth") notes (for some fills or double bass maybe) we can actually get 16 of them in the same measure because one 1/4 note is made up of four 1/16 notes and we can fit a total of four 1/4 notes in one measure. The same goes for 1/2, 1/8, and 1/32 notes and so on. The note value is also important for setting up your MIDI editor in order to program your beats because it determines what value you have to set the grid to. If you want to program 1/16 notes you'll also have to set the grid to that or otherwise you'd just have to eyeball it, and that probably doesn't make for good results.

Time, time signature, or meter: As mentioned above we mostly deal with 4/4 time in today's music. This means that one measure is made up of a total of four 1/4 notes (or eight 1/8 notes and so on). Again, you need this in order to set up your DAW and the grid correctly. The first number in the time signature determines how many beats fit into one measure, while the second number determines the kind of beats. If you are numbers savvy you've probably realized that 4/4 is the same as 8/8 or 16/16 or even 1/1. Technically these are nothing but fractions that all have the same solution: 1. So either way you'd be able to fit in the same number of notes in each measure. However it has become common practice to use the note value that drives the beat as the second number in the equation (or the "denominator" to speak in mathematical terms). Since we are just so used to counting "One, two, three, four... one, two, three, four..." when we play our favorite riffs, this is just the naming convention that established itself for practicality reasons. Of course, there can be other meters like 3/4 and 6/8 (which are basically the same) as well. I'll discuss them in the corresponding bonus chapter.

Tempo: The last variable to determine a beat is the tempo. It is measured in beats per minute, or BPM for short. For example, a tempo of 120 BPM would fit 120 beats into one minute and therefore each beat would last 0.5 seconds (60 seconds divided by 120 beats). But what note value do these have? Once again, the time signature helps us out here. The second number always determines the note value of the indicated tempo. So, 4/4 time at a 120 BPM means that there are 120 1/4 notes each minute (and four of them in each measure respectively as explained above).

If that was a little confusing to you, don't worry about it too much. You'll get a grip on things soon as we start programming our first beats. Speaking of which: here we go!

Four to the floor

You've probably realized that drummer's in today's music mostly alternate between Bass drum and Snare drum. Thereby the Bass drum goes on beats one and three and the Snare drum goes on beats two and four of each measure respectively. This is probably the single most important beat principle to know. If you are just looking for something to jam along to or to just get an idea of how your riff will sound with drums this is the way to go. This beat will fit with 99% of the music that you can come up with (as long as it's set in 4/4 time). I'm not saying it'll be the best fit ever, but it will work.

To program it for yourself, set the time signature to 4/4 (that will most likely be the standard setting in your DAW anyway) and the grid to 1/4 notes. Create a MIDI event as described above and open it in your DAW's MIDI editor. Click on the grid using the pencil tool (or similar) and position Bass drum and Snare drum as described above. It should look something like this.

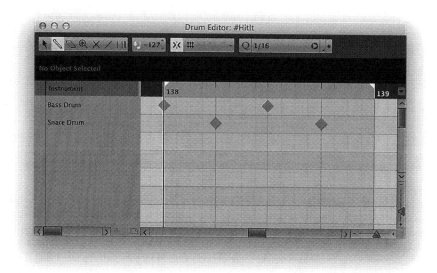

Figure 5: Bass drum on beats one and three, Snare drum on beats two and four

There is also a variation of this beat with a Bass drum hit on each of the four beats. Just four Bass drum hits on their own (without the Snare drum on top of it) are called a "Four to the Floor", because there are four Bass drum hits: one on every count of the measure. Since the Bass drum is standing on the floor, someone came up with the clever name for this beat. This beat get's a lot of use in mainstream Pop music. Sometimes these songs will use just the Bass drum. They may also feature additional Snare drum hits and sometimes the Snare drum will even be substituted or supported with a Clap sound.

Figure 6: The famous "Four to the floor" beat with additional Snare drum hits

Note: Usually the tempo would be an important thing to consider as well, since not all beats shine in every tempo. But since this is such a basic beat, it's an exception to this rule and always works. Start with 120 BPM if you like.

You might have noticed the little bars at the bottom of the grid in this last screenshot. These represent the velocities of the hits on the grid and determine how loud a drum sound is played. They play a crucial role in making any beat sound realistic. Therefore, they will be covered in detail in a dedicated chapter later in this book. For now we will focus on the actual writing of drumbeats, so just make sure that every hit you program has at least a velocity of 100, preferably 127. It doesn't matter if all beats have the same velocity for now. In fact, it will even sound robotic but right now we just need to learn the principles of beats. We'll find out how to make them sound more natural later on. To make sure all your hits are at the same velocities, select all of them on the grid and modify the bars right below the grid so that they are as high as it gets with the pencil tool (or similar). In addition to that, you should also set the default velocity for programmed hits to the same value so that you don't have to go in and change it every time. Usually, this only requires you to enter the desired value in a textbox or choose it from a dropdown menu within the MIDI editor. Please check your

DAW's manual to find out how to perform that action. For now I will omit velocities in screenshots altogether.

Congratulations, you are now qualified to program drums for the majority of Pop artists on the Billboard charts! Seriously, check out Katy Perry, Miley Cyrus, and whoever is topping the charts right now and you will hear this beat over, and over again.

Even if you're more into Rock and Heavy music, you'll soon realize that the same principles apply. There will most likely be more variations on the Bass drum and Snare drum work, but for the most part, there will be a Bass drum on beats one and three and a Snare drum on beats two and four. I always use this as a starting point and expand my beats from there.

Now, if you've listened closely (especially to more guitar-oriented Pop, Rock, and of course Heavy music) you probably feel like the little beat above doesn't yet sound quite right. Seems like it's missing something. You are right. In an every day song context Bass drum and Snare drum are usually accompanied by some kind of cymbal. Remember what I wrote about the smallest possible drum kit in the section about the kit pieces? Let's place a closed Hi-hat on each of the four hits in this beat and see how that sounds.

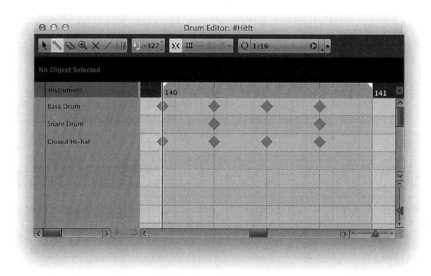

Figure 7: Four to the floor with added Hi-hat

Now you've got a real beat. There are many more options for the accompanying element, though. The Hi-hat alone gives you two more (open and pedal), and you could also use the Ride cymbal or a Crash cymbal to go along with Bass and Snare drum. Sometimes it also benefits the part to use a Floor Tom instead of a cymbal. You could even pair it up with the Hi-hat (being played using its pedal) for a total of four elements in the beat. Try all these different options to hear for yourself how they affect the feel of the groove. Make sure to delete any previous experiments with other elements first though, because drummers may be a lot of things but there is one thing they are not. Read on to the next section to find out what.

A drummer is not an Octopus

Unlike an Octopus that has eight arms, a drummer only has two arms and two legs. Using his limbs, he can hit four pieces of the drum kit at any given time. Options are further restricted by the fact that only two kit pieces can be played with feet, namely the Hi-hat and the Bass drum. The rest need to be hit with sticks. Whenever you are trying to come up with a groove, try and be aware of that, in order to create a beat that could realistically be played by a real drummer. The easiest and safest way to make sure you are on the right track is slowing down the groove in your head and trying to air-drum it. That's right, just picture a drum kit in front of you and try to recreate what you just put down on the grid in mid-air. If you find yourself trying to hit two Toms, the Snare and the Ride cymbal at the same time it's save to say that it's time to go back to the drawing board (i.e. the MIDI editor).

That being said, I sometimes do incorporate "impossible" elements in my grooves. However, I try and keep them to a minimum. For example, I might add an extra cymbal even though I've already run out of virtual hands for extra impact. If the song calls for an even more drastic approach, I would most likely create an additional drum track just for effect drums (which makes more sense for mixing as well). These kinds of methods are only needed in progressive Rock or different kinds of Metal music though. For the first genre we are going to look at in detail, we'll be dealing with simpler beats.

Pop

Even though generally speaking beats in Pop music might be simple compared to other genres, there is still a great deal we need to know in order to serve the individual song we are working on as good as we can. That's because for the most part, drums are not the forefront of any given Pop song.

I've written it earlier and I still stand by it: If you understood what I wrote in the "Four to the floor" section of this book and if you are able to apply it to your Pop songs, you are already half-way there. The reason for that is that in modern Pop music, the singer's voice is the most important element of the song. All the other instruments are just there to support the voice so that it can shine in their light. Just listen to your favorite Pop record and you will notice that there is a special production-emphasis on certain effects, harmonies, etc. on the main vocal, and that it's melody is probably what's still echoing in your head hours after you've heard the song. The drums? Not so much. Now what does that mean for us as virtual drummers? Simple. We have to make sure to stay in the background and to not overdo our parts so that the vocals can catch the listeners' attention. This actually sounds easier than it may be for some, so let's see how we can benefit the song.

> *Before we start a quick side note on the term "Pop": There's lots of different music out there and while a lot of it might be labeled Pop it doesn't necessarily have a whole lot in common. Or would you say Miley Cyrus, Katy Perry and Britney Spears compare well to acts like Bloc Party, Editors, or The Killers? Probably not and neither would I. While the first group is definitely well suited for having*

their drums programmed, the latter isn't so much. These artists probably wouldn't even think about programming their drums as they work in a band-context and don't rely on a producer to do his magic so much. If you still find yourself having to program drums for this kind of music, you should also take a look at the "Rock" section since a lot of the stuff that's discussed there will probably help you as well. I'm not saying this section is limited to mainstream Solo Artists, but what is discussed as "Pop" here is definitely more oriented towards straightforward, easy to listen to music with great melodies. Also, make sure to check out the Chapter on Humanization and apply the information given there to the beats of this section for the most realistic results.

Building the beat

Let's take another look at the basic beat from the last chapter.

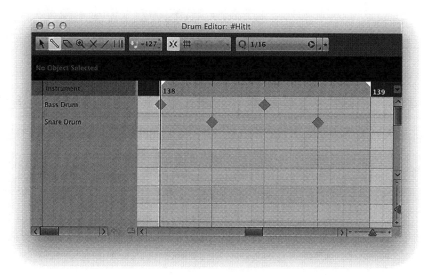

Figure 8: Bass drum on beats one and three, Snare drum on beats two and four

We placed the Bass drum on beats one and three and the Snare drums on beats two and four here. This will be our starting point for all the beats in this section, so let's see how we can build from here. Assuming this basic beat structure is all we need for the song we are working on, we can now look at all the options we have to occupy the imaginary drummer's second hitting hand. If you remember the section about the pieces of a drum kit, you will know that the most basic drum kit is made up of Bass drum, Snare drum, and Hi-hat. So let's start with that.

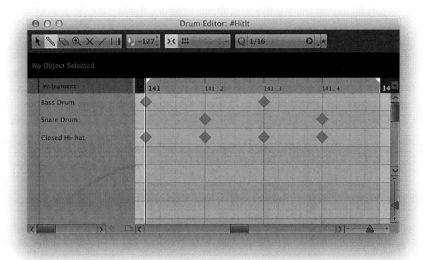

Figure 9: Simple beat with three elements

Ok, to be honest, that still doesn't sound like much. Granted it got a little more interesting with the addition of the Hi-hat but it's not that big of a leap from what we started with. What if we tried an open Hi-hat sound?

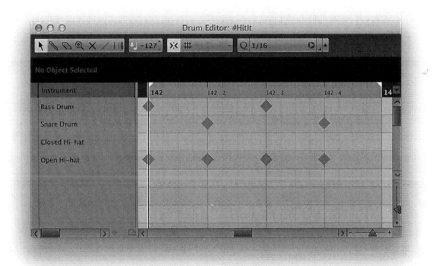

Figure 10: Simple beat with an open Hi-hat sound instead of a closed one

Now we're starting to roll. We can definitely hear how this has a more "rocking" feel to it than just the closed Hi-hat that may even have been hard to hear over the Bass drum and the Snare drum. The groove we've just programmed is sort of driving and even heavy, if you will. This is because of the emphasis on all of the four beats in this measure. For a little more of a laid-back feel set you grid to 1/8 notes and try the following.

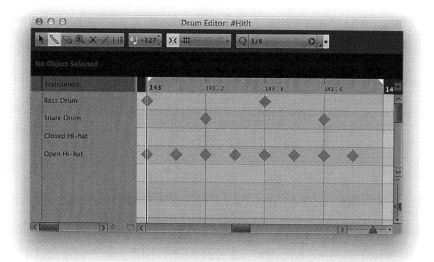

Figure 11: 1/8 notes on open Hi-hat

This definitely feels lighter than the last one and goes perfectly with some guitar chords strummed in an 1/8-note-rhythm-pattern during a build-up pre-chorus or even in a chorus itself.

What if your song has a more "dance-y" feel to it? Try putting the Hi-hat on the off-beat.

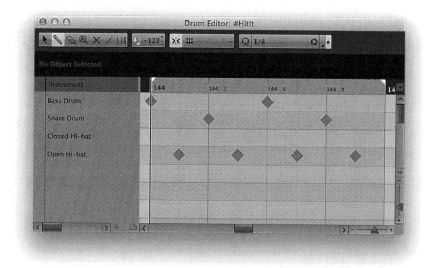

Figure 12: Open Hi-hat on off-beat

Sounds good, doesn't it? For a less prominent beat, you can also use a closed Hi-hat sound instead of the open one.

Another Hi-hat variation that you can use to spice up your rhythms is based on 1/16 notes. Set the grid of your MIDI editor to 1/16 notes to be able to program this pattern.

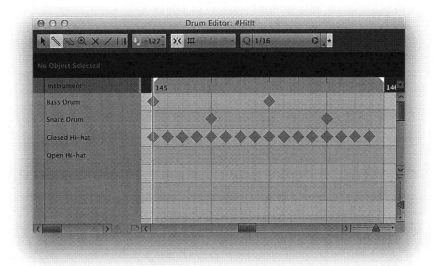

Figure 13: Closed Hi-hat pattern using 1/16 notes

With this you can tag along to a guitar riff that incorporates a lot of 1/16 notes or drive the grove in a faster direction just with the drums alone. You can also use the open Hi-hat sound for this rhythm. Or better yet: Use a combination of the two. As you know, the Hi-hat can be operated and modified using its pedal. A real drummer can do this while he plays so we are free to make use of that in our beats as well. Try and mix it up, and maybe throw in an open Hi-hat at the end of each group of four Hi-hat hits like in the following example.

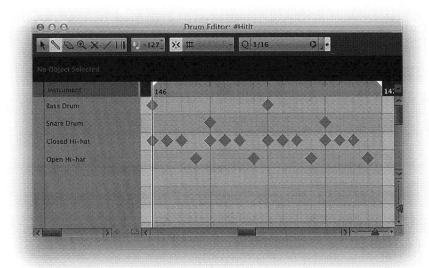

Figure 14: Using two different Hi-hat sounds in one pattern

If your drum software offers different Hi-hat samples, make use of them. That way you can vary how much the Hi-hat is opened up and make the sound a lot more realistic.

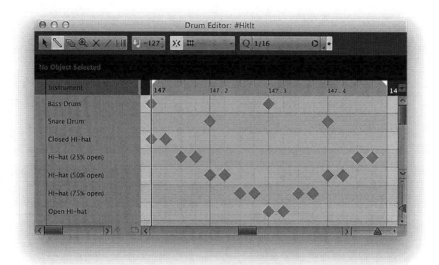

Figure 15: Hi-hat pattern with various opening degrees

On this beat, the Hi-hat get's opened up (and closed down again after that) a little more after every two hits like the drummer is constantly moving the Hi-hat pedal. This not only keeps the pattern interesting, but it's a great option to create build-up towards a new section of a song as well. To create that sort of feel instead of closing the Hi-hat back down, extend the opening-up-period before you head to the next section of the song. Of course you don't have to use that particular sequence of opening steps. You could just as well go from 25% open to 50% open, back to 25% open again and so forth. Just try different variations and use what sounds best to you and what fits your song.

You are also free to break up the Hi-hat rhythm in whatever way you like. Don't think you have to play 1/4, 1/8, or 1/16 notes all the way through. By not limiting yourself to such rigid rhythm constructs you can open up a whole new slew of possibilities. With your grid set to 1/16 notes and any underlying combination of Bass drum and Snare drum beats, try throwing in Hi-hats all over the place and see what kind of effects you can get. Here is an example that involves different variations on each of the four beats in this measure. You are free to stick to the same variation for every beat of the measure or add in even more variation by using different patterns in the following measures. Try different combinations until you find something that creates the feel that you are trying to achieve.

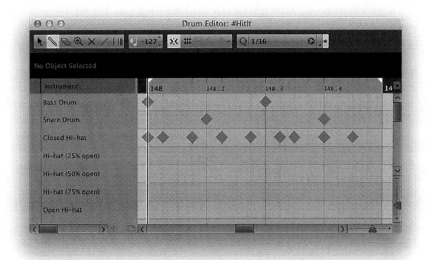

Figure 16: Varying Hi-hat pattern

Generally speaking, try experimenting with opening/closing and breaking up the Hi-hat a little more. You'll immediately notice how it breathes more life into your grooves and makes them more realistic. If you listen closely you'll find that drummers use all kinds of variations with this technique so there really isn't any wrong (or right for that matter) way to do it. Just experiment. Also, be advised that you don't have to use the same open/close and rhythm pattern throughout a whole section of a song. You can just throw in some variation at whatever point it fits. Open/close and rhythm variations can also be used leading up to a fill, or instead of it leading up to a new section of a song. It doesn't have to be recurring over and over again. Just because we are programming our drum tracks, doesn't mean we have to keep them repetitive. With these tools at our hands, there's really no excuse not to try and make use of them as best we can. Another way to use the Hi-hat to place accents on certain beats is discussed in the next paragraph.

Hi-hat barking

The Hi-hat being hit while open and closed quickly afterwards is revered to as Hi-hat barking. It can be used to place some sort of "stop-emphasize" on certain hits. In order to achieve this, we need an open Hi-hat sound and a sound of the Hi-hat being closed with the pedal. The latter might be called "Pedal Chick" or similar in your drum software. These two sounds work together to produce the desired effect. First we need to hit the open Hi-hat, and then immediately afterwards we need to put the sound of the Hi-hat being closed with the pedal. It depends on the tempo of the song how soon after the open hit we have to place the closing one but try an 1/8, a 1/16, or even a 1/32 note after the open hit. If all else fails you can even turn off the grid and move the closing hit around freely until you like the sound. Here is an example of this technique used in a beat. This works great at around 120 BPM.

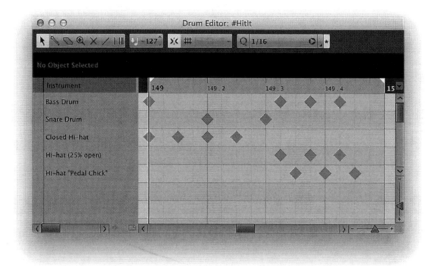

Figure 17: Hi-hat barking

You'll notice that I used the "Hit-hat (25% open)" sound in the above example. That just so happens to sound best for this technique with my drum software. Experiment with the open Hi-hat sounds that your drum software provides and choose whichever you like best.

Of course, you are not limited to using your Hi-hat to accompany your Bass drum and Snare drum. Try the Toms for a change.

Tom beats

For more quite verses or middle sections, we can try to use the Floor Tom instead of the Hi-hat. Set the grid to 1/8 notes again and put a Floor Tom hit on every 1/8 throughout the measure. It should look something like this.

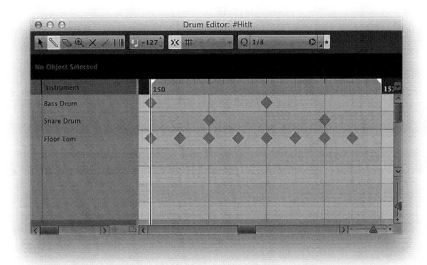

Figure 18: Floor Tom acting as an accompanying element (instead of the Hi-hat)

I like to add a little variation to this rhythm at the end of each section where the two 1/16 notes are played on the Floor Tom. Set your grid to 1/16 notes to recreate this groove.

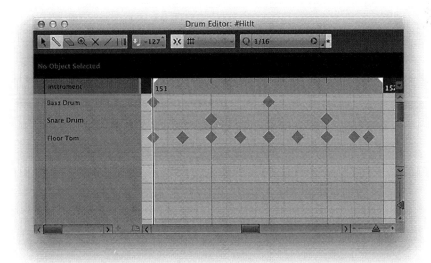

Figure 19: Floor Tom acting as an accompanying element (variation)

With this rhythm, we are using both our drummer's hands for the Snare drum and the Floor Tom, but only one of his feet for the Bass drum. Let's use his other foot on the Hi-hat pedal. If your drum software offers some sort of "Foot Splash" or "Pedal Chick" samples, these are the ones to use here. Otherwise, regular open and closed hits will work as well. If you are using open and closed hits, this will make for an "impossible" drum part, because the drummer's hands are already occupied. Since your intension is to mimic a Hi-hat that's played just using the pedal, a little cheating is fine in this case.

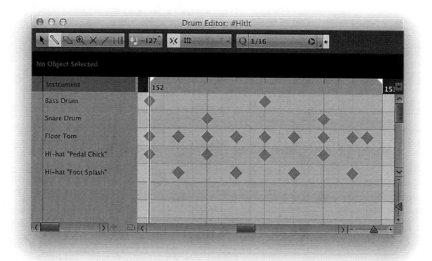

Figure 20: Floor Tom and Hi-hat both acting as accompanying elements

With all the stuff that's going on, this is kind of a "lively" rhythm. If that's too much for your particular song, try cutting out the foot splashes and using just the pedal chicks. Or, just leave out the Hi-hat altogether. Just because we can, doesn't mean we have to use all the limbs a drummer has.

Here are a few more complex Tom-based beats.

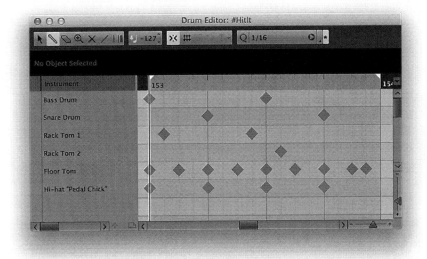

Figure 21: Grid: 1/16 notes, Appropriate tempo: 70-140 BPM

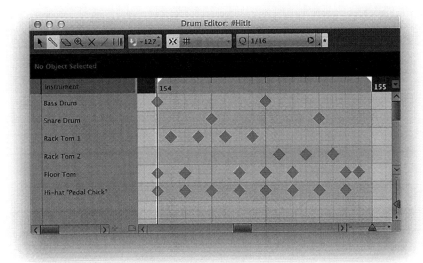

Figure 22: Grid: 1/16 notes, Appropriate tempo: 70-140 BPM

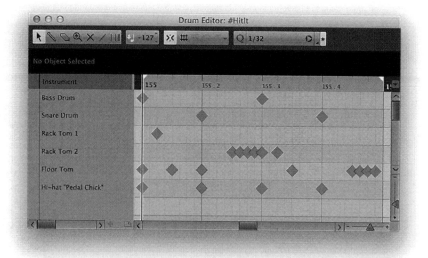

Figure 23: Grid: 1/32 notes, Appropriate tempo: 80-110 BPM

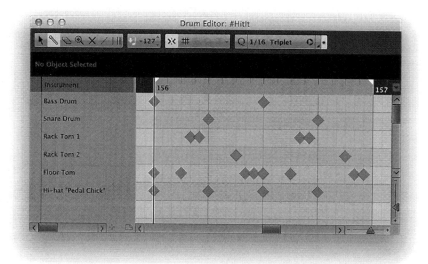

Figure 24: Grid: 1/16 note triplets, Appropriate tempo: 65-95 BPM

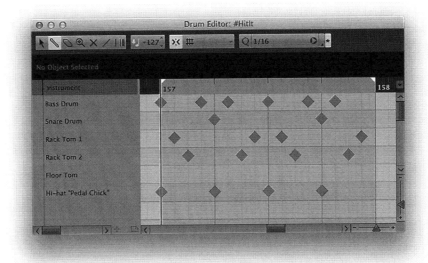

Figure 25: Grid: 1/16 notes, Appropriate tempo: 70-120 BPM (up to 140 BPM for a Metal song)

If these are too heavy for what you are looking, for try the technique described in the next section.

Sidestick

If you need to cut back dynamically on certain sections of a song, try exchanging the Snare with a "Side stick" or "Cross Stick" sound (or whatever it may be called in your drum software). To produce this sound, the drummer doesn't hit the Snare drum's head, but its Rim. Therefore, the sound is less powerful and has a totally different feel – it's very "clicky" and brazen. You can try exchanging the Snare drum for the Sidestick in all the grooves from above. You can also experiment with grooves that feature the Sidestick more prominently than the Snare drum like the following two.

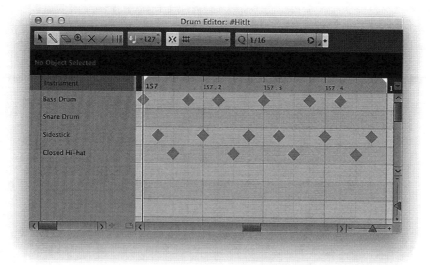

Figure 26: Grid: 1/16 notes, Appropriate tempo: 70-110 BPM

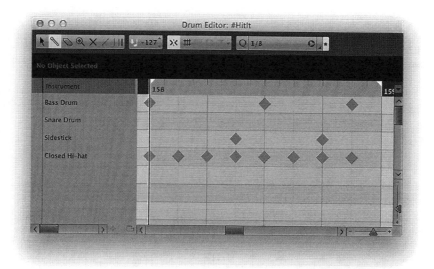

Figure 27: Grid: 1/8 notes, Appropriate tempo: 90-165 BPM

Something like the above examples goes particularly well at the end of a section where you used the Sidestick as a replacement for the Snare drum on a more straightforward groove. Here's another example.

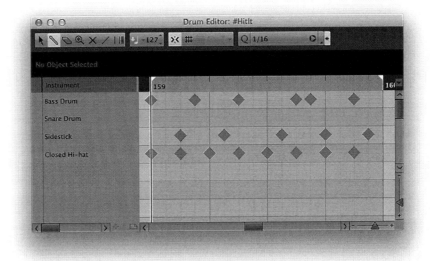

Figure 28: Grid: 1/16 notes, Appropriate tempo: 80-120 BPM

The Sidestick is especially suited to the technique described in the following section.

Half-time feel

If you are working on a ballad or more generally a song that requires a slower feel try a half-time groove. Instead of starting with the Bass drum and the Snare drum on beats one and three and two and four respectively, put the Bass drum on beat one and the Snare drum on beat three. This turns out to be the same thing as if you were to program beats as you are used to, but the tempo was slowed down to half its original value (thus the term "half-time").

Using this principle, all the beats discussed in this book can easily be changed into half-time grooves if need be. You can then add additional elements in the newly created free space. For starters, try adding some Toms or double the amount of accompanying element hits.

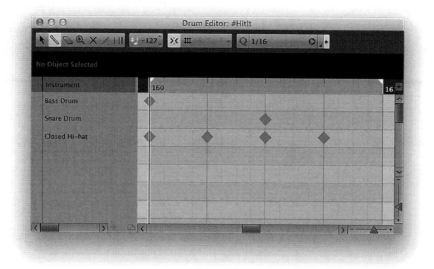

Figure 29: A basic half-time feel beat

The Ride cymbal

So far we've covered beats supported by a lot of variations of Hi-hat and (Floor) Tom options. There's one more supporting element that get's quite a lot of use in Pop music, and that is the Ride cymbal. Your drum software should at least offer "Bow" and "Bell" hits, and maybe even "Edge" hits. While the latter is too heavy for Pop music, most of the time the bow and bell come in quite handy. I like to use the bow hits on 1/4 and 1/8 notes whilst keeping the bell to 1/4 notes, since it tends to be irritating if overused. To me, the Ride cymbal comes in handy on Pre-Choruses and Choruses and middle sections. For some reason I don't use it all that much during Verses, but that doesn't mean you shouldn't give it a try. You can try the 1/4 and 1/8 note rhythm patterns we've used for the Hi-hat above for the Ride cymbal as well. Personally, I never found much use for the 1/16-note-pattern on it. Putting the Bell just on the off-beat is another option that adds an especially outstanding emphasis to your groove. Make sure to give it a try.

Bass drum variations

Another element that can be varied for a different groove feel is the Bass drum. So far we've only used it on beats one and three in this chapter. For a faster feel, it can also be added to one or both of the off beats of these beats. Here are the three variations that result from that.

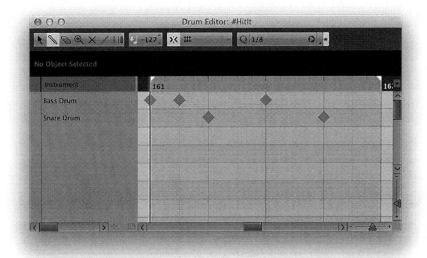

Figure 30: Bass drum variation one

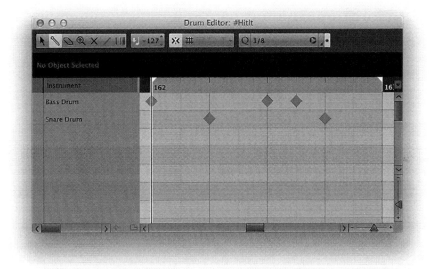

Figure 31: Bass drum variation two

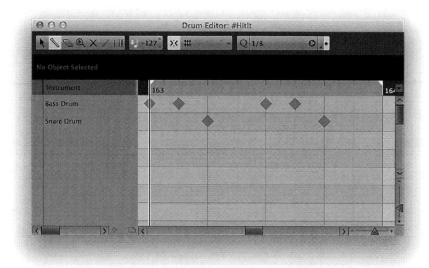

Figure 32: Bass drum variation three

Combine these with the supporting element of your choice (Hi-hat, Ride cymbal or Floor Tom) to complete the groove, or use them on their own for effect in a special part of your song.

Of course there can be other variations for the Bass drum as well. But as I mentioned earlier, in Pop music, all the instruments should stay in the background so that the vocals can really shine. That's why we'll leave it at that, as far as the Bass drum is concerned.

We may have to add some build-ups, transitions, or fills to our drum tracks to glue the individual sections of our song together. These will be discussed in the following section. We'll keep them easy and to a minimum for the reason given above. For more elaborate explanations of fills, please refer to the "Rock" chapter.

Pop fills

A basic fill will typically be made up of 1/8 or 1/16 notes played by the Toms in some way. The most common is usually groups of four. Make sure that your grid is set to 1/16 notes in order to be able to program these fills.

In this groove, the first two beats are part of the original groove of the song, while beats three and four represent the fill.

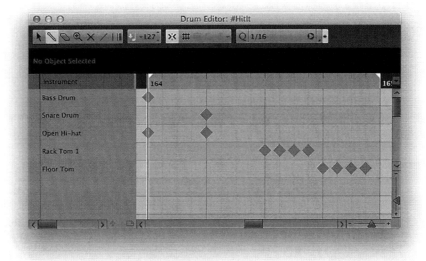

Figure 33: Simple fill using groups of four on the Toms

If you want a shorter fill you can just use groups of two Tom hits on beat four.

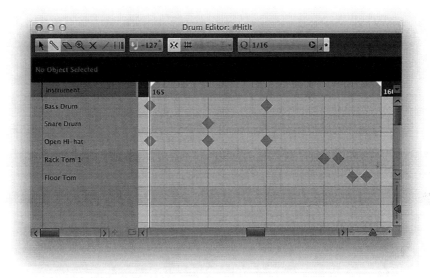

Figure 34: Simple fill using groups of two on the Toms

You can also incorporate the Snare drum like in the following example.

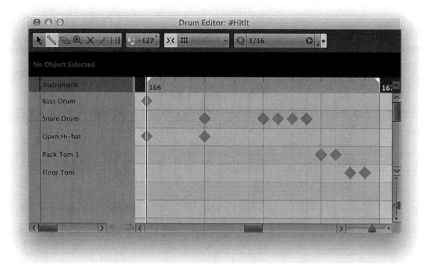

Figure 35: Simple fill using the Snare drum and the Toms

Of course there is also a shorter version that includes the Snare drum.

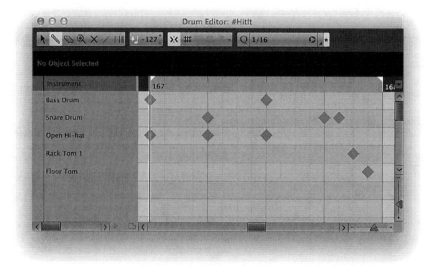

Figure 36: Simple fill using the Snare drum and the Toms (variation)

Here's a little variation that incorporates the Bass drum as well.

Figure 37: Simple fill using the Snare drum, the Toms, and the Bass drum

It's also possible to use just the Snare drum to create a fill.

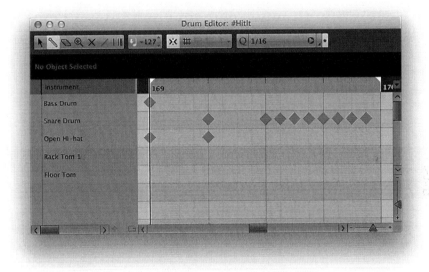

Figure 38: Snare drum fill

Here's the short version.

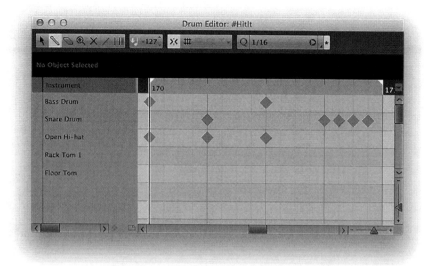

Figure 39: Snare drum fill (variation)

Furthermore, all of these can be "slowed down" by simply using just half the hits. So instead of 1/16 notes, use 1/8 notes -- but only half as many. Give it a try and see how it affects the feel of the groove and how you can incorporate it into your drum tracks.

These examples of fills should give you an idea of what's possible, but don't limit yourself. Experiment with different rhythms and elements (Toms, Snare drum, Bass drum), keeping in mind not to include too many hits at the same time that a real drummer wouldn't be able to play.

One more important element that's used to transition between sections of songs is what I call a "Build-up". By that I mean a drum part that slowly increases its intensity. In this section we will use a combination of the Snare drum and the Floor Tom. Your grid should be set to 1/8 notes.

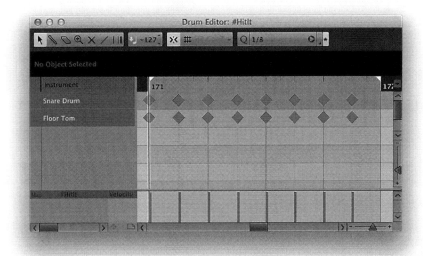

Figure 40: Build-up using the Snare drum and the Floor Tom

If you've tried programming this for yourself, you'll understand the idea behind it but you also realized that it doesn't sound very good. There is no build-up at all, because everything is the same volume. This is where we have to start playing with velocities for the first time. You may have noticed the bars below the grid. These are the velocity levels for all individual hits in the grid above. If you select a certain hit its corresponding velocity bar will light up as well letting you know which hit it belongs to. The higher the bar, the louder the corresponding drum hit is. Since we want to create build up, we have to slowly increase the volume of the hits. Your DAW may or may not have tools to support you in the process (please refer to its manual) but you can easily do it yourself. Just select all the drum hits (Snare drum and the Floor Tom) and modify the velocity bar using your DAW's pencil tool (or similar). Make sure that the velocity bars form somewhat of an upward curve from left to right. The end result should look something like this.

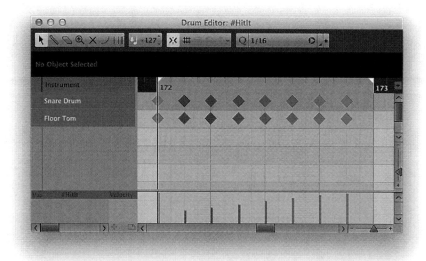

Figure 41: Build-up using the Snare drum and the Floor Tom (modified velocities)

Now that sounds better, doesn't it? Notice that I've left the first hit at the original velocity to start of the build-up with a "Bang" so to speak and then go to a low velocity immediately on the second hit. If it better suits your song, you can start with low a velocity on the first hit already.

Here's another variation of the build-up incorporating the Bass drum and the Hi-hat (played with the pedal) as well.

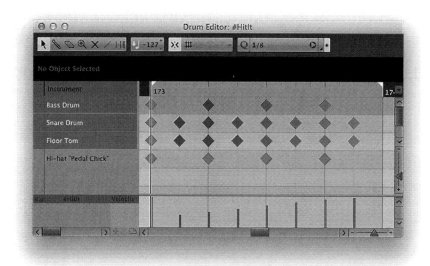

Figure 42: Build-up using multiple elements

In the previous example, you can't see all the velocity bars since they are overlapping and different ones are visible in the MIDI editor depending on which drum hits are selected, but the color of the hits on the grid gives you a good understanding of what was done there, velocity-wise. You can see that the first hit is once again the loudest, and that it includes Bass drum and the Hi-hat this time. Going further, the Bass drum is played on beats two, three, and four and the velocity was adjusted to match the velocities of the Snare drum and Tom. Notice the purple colored hits that turn more and more red the louder the individual hits are. For the Hi-hat, I decided to stick with a loud volume throughout the whole build-up, because it seems it would be very hard for a drummer to achieve different volume levels when just using his foot on the Hi-hat pedal. Also, the Hi-hat pedal sound isn't very loud most of the time so it might be a good idea to keep it louder anyway in order to make sure it can be heard over the rest of the drums.

Please note that this was just a quick introduction to velocities, to achieve the build-up. Make sure to check out the chapter on Humanization for more detailed techniques to create realistic sounding drum beats. For now, we will revert back to fixed velocities in order to focus on the actual writing of drum parts rather then the optimizing process.

Crash cymbals and final tips

Important elements of the drum kit that we have neglected completely so far are the Crash cymbals. As I've mentioned earlier, their primary role is to put accents on certain parts of the song. These include, but are not limited to: a new measure, a chord change or a new part of the song (Verse, Chorus, etc.). As I've also mentioned earlier in Pop music, the instruments should rather support the vocals than stand out on their own. Therefore, Crash cymbals should only be used sparingly. While they're often used in heavier genres like Rock and Metal, it's a safer bet to use them just when a new part of the song comes in. That being said, you shouldn't be afraid to place a cymbal here and there every once in a while, when you feel the overall arrangement would benefit from it. Just keep "the big picture" in mind at all times.

Most drum kits feature two Crash cymbals. Some drummers will hit them both at the same time for added impact, so you can do that as well. Just remember that a drummer is no Octopus and remove anything else you might have going on on this particular hit that a real drummer wouldn't be able to play. Of course, using just one Crash cymbal at a time is fine as well.

As professional as a lot of drum software may sound, Crash cymbal samples often make the difference between good and bad sounding (programmed) drum tracks. If you happen to be unhappy with the Crash cymbals that you have at hand, open up the mixer of your drum software and lower the faders of the channels marked "Overheads" (and maybe the ones labeled "Room" as well) a little bit to lower the volume of the Crash cymbals in your overall drum sound. You can find more on mixing tips in the corresponding bonus chapter.

Another way to convey to the listener that they are now listening to another part of the song is by changing up the accompanying element. As mentioned earlier, options include the Hi-hat (opened, closed, and played with its pedal), the Ride cymbal, and the Toms. Depending on what element you decide to use and whether you use a groove based on 1/4 or 1/8 notes, the overall feel of the drum track will change. Closed Hi-hats generally make for a pretty straightforward groove, while the Ride cymbal sounds more "open" and therefore does very well in Pre-Choruses and Choruses. The Hi-hat played with the pedal often goes together with a Tom-based groove. This makes for a "stompy" feel. Last but not least, the open Hi-hat adds a rocking, forward-pushing drive to a song section.

Speaking of rocking grooves, head over to the next section to kick it up a notch and find out everything about Rock drums.

Rock

In contrast to Pop music where the vocals should be the most important part of any song, Rock music is typically more of a band thing. All the instruments and the vocals work together to create powerful pieces of music that we all love. Each musician in a Rock band is supposed to add his or her own personal flavor to the music so that the band becomes a very distinctive entity. This is good news, because finally we can get a little more creative as well. No longer do we have to keep the drums in the background. Now it's their time to shine as well.

In my opinion, what really drives a song forward the most is when all the instruments groove together. For example, the main guitar riff follows a certain rhythm and the bass, and more importantly the drums keep up with that same rhythm. This is what I call "locking-in" the drums with the other elements of a song. What do we do that if we are supposed to keep the Bass drum on beats one and three, and the Snare drum on beats two and four you ask? Simple – we just add additional hits.

Since this is different on a song-by-song basis, it's hard to give any concrete examples, but this is how you can *lock-in* your drum tracks with existing music:

1. Find out what element in the arrangement drives the main rhythm of your song. In Rock music, most of the time this will be the guitar(s), but it can also be the bass or even the vocals. Also, keep in mind that this can change throughout the different parts of the song. The verse might move around a special guitar riff, while the chorus is clearly driven by the vocals. If you are not sure about which element in the arrangement to hold

on to, try the guitar(s) first. If they are playing just plain 1/4 or 1/8 notes throughout the whole section look for the next best element that incorporates a more varying rhythm.

2. This might be hard for beginners: select a closed Hi-hat sample and try to recreate the rhythm of the element you chose in step #1 in your MIDI editor. If you are having a hard time figuring out the rhythm, try "learning" it first buy just clapping along to the guitar (or whatever) riff with your hands. Once you can clap it you can then slow it down in your head and slowly piece it together one hit after another. It might also help you to keep the metronome going in your Recording Software for another point of reference throughout this process.

3. Once you've programmed the rhythm of the driving element using just closed Hi-hat samples, it's time to make a real beat out of it. For starters add the Bass drum on beats one and three and the Snare drum on beats two and four like we are already used to. Now add more Bass drum hits to all the other Hi-hats, except for the ones already occupied by the Snare drum. See what you did there? You just transferred the rhythm of the driving element into a Bass and Snare drum pattern. Great Job!

4. With this last step, it's time to remove the initial Hi-hat hits. We don't need them anymore, since the Bass drum and the Snare drum have taken over. After deleting them, we are left with nothing but the Bass drum and the Snare drum. You are now free to add whatever accompanying element (Hi-hat, Ride, or Toms) you see fit. Make sure to put it in a straight rhythm (1/4 or 1/8 notes or another pattern I've discussed in the Pop section of this book) though. This is going to be the reference point for where the actual beat is. You don't want that to be all over the place together with the main rhythm driver, Bass and Snare drums.

And there you have it – you have just successfully locked-in your drums with the main rhythm of your song.

Snare drum Comping

To take the concept of locking-in the drums with the main rhythm of the song even further, drummers have come to use what is referred to as Snare drum Comping. This is actually a technique that was first used in Jazz music, where the drummer would listen to what the other musicians were playing and then try to ac*comp*any or *comp*lement that, hence the name. This is essentially what we just did with the Bass drum. You can now go and try it the exact opposite way, leaving the Bass drum on beats one and three constantly and filling the rest of the hits with the Snare drum. Depending on the riff you are trying to lock-in with, this might sound weird, though. In order to avoid this, try incorporating a mixed approach and using the Bass drum and the Snare drum alike. Again, this really depends on the individual case. Generally speaking, the Snare becomes useful when you want to put accents on certain hits, while the Bass drum can cover the remaining beats.

If you are struggling to understand the concepts I just illustrated, go listen to two of my favorite pieces of modern Rock music that incorporate these techniques. I'm sure you'll get a better understanding once hearing it. You'll also notice how powerful this can be. The songs I recommend to check out are *Jimmy Eat World*'s "Big Casino" (from their 2007 album "Chase this Light") and *Thirty Seconds to Mars*' "Kings and Queens" (from their 2009 album "This is War"). Pay special attention to the intros and choruses, and you'll know what I'm talking about instantly.

Once again, this highly individual technique can't be explained by just showing off a number of pre-written grooves that you could easily copy for your songs. There will be times where you can just resort to the grooves that I've discussed in the Pop section and you'll be totally fine. If you struggle with locking-in your drums with other elements of the arrangement, don't despair. You'll get a hold of it eventually once you've gained a little more experience.

Like I said, this technique can't be generalized. Regardless, I'd like to give you a couple of groove examples that you can try and re-create using your drum software as a starting point. Keep in mind though they are highly unlikely to fit your music right away and that they are just meant to be a starting point. The first example spans over two measures.

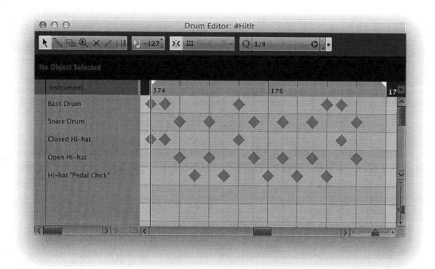

Figure 43: Grid: 1/8 notes, Appropriate tempo: 100-160 BPM

Notice how I opened up the Hi-hat for added impact on all the Snare drum hits. You can leave out the Hi-hat barks for a more open feel.

Here's another one.

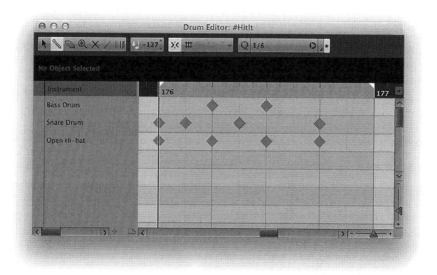

Figure 44: Grid: 1/8 notes, Appropriate tempo: 100-160 BPM

Another technique to enhance a groove that's very popular in Rock music is the use of Ghost notes.

Ghost notes

Ghost notes refer to notes that are played on the Snare drum in-between the regular Snare drum hits (usually on beats two and four as explained above) usually one 1/16 note earlier or later. But in contrast to the regular hits, ghost notes are not as loud. Their main purpose is to break up an otherwise rigid groove and make it seem livelier. They are more "felt" than actually heard, especially when the whole band is playing.

In order to be able to program them realistically, we have to use what we've learned about velocities above, and lower the velocity on the ghost hits. I'll go over the details on velocity in the Humanizing chapter. For now, just eyeball it and lower the velocity on the ghost hits as you see fit. Naturally the ghost notes will be louder on faster tempos as the drummer has to move faster, and therefore even the softer hits will be a little bit louder than on a slow groove. Here are two examples of grooves enhanced with ghost notes.

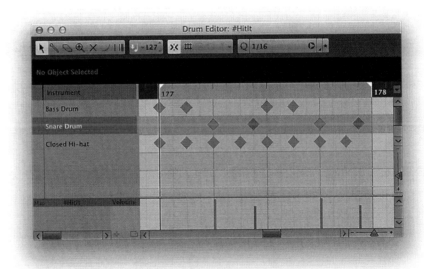

Figure 45: Grid: 1/16 notes, Appropriate tempo: 85-125 BPM

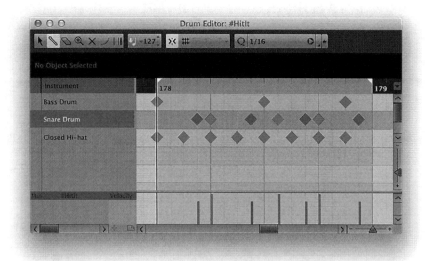

Figure 46: Grid: 1/16 notes, Appropriate tempo: 85-125 BPM

When experimenting with ghost notes, try placing hits one 1/16 note (or depending on the tempo 1/8 or 1/32 note) before or after a regular Bass or Snare drum hit. You can also combine ghost hits before and after regular hits. You can take this to the extreme by adding ghost notes before and after every single hit. Who knows, there might be occasions where that seems to fit. Experiment with different variations. Here's the "Full on" variant.

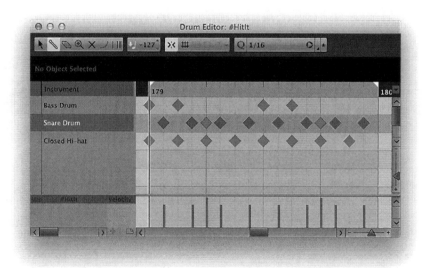

Figure 47: Grid: 1/16 notes, Appropriate tempo: 85-125 BPM

This is a great way to breath life into an otherwise simple groove. If you were just starting out as a real drummer, this would probably take you weeks, if not months to master. As a programmer, you can incorporate this technique with ease.

The Ride cymbal

In modern Rock, the Ride cymbal plays a more prominent role compared to Pop. Next to its regular "Ping" and Bell sounds, it can also be hit very hard to produce a Crash-like sound. The naming of these sounds will vary across different drum software. Try looking for "Ride Edge" sounds. If you can't find any with that name in your drum software, just trust your ears and use the Ride sound that closest resembles a Crash sound.

Why do we need that sound if we already have Crashes, anyway? While the Ride cymbal being hit hard on its Edge somewhat resembles the sound of a Crash cymbal, it's still not the same. Like I mentioned earlier, due to its bigger size, the Ride cymbal has less Attack than a Crash cymbal. Therefore, it produces a less pronounced sound than a Crash cymbal. This is especially useful if you need to make it sound heavy, as if there's a lot going on drum-wise, and still keep it somewhat in the background. Use this sound as an alternative to the Hi-hat, Toms, or other Ride sounds as your accompanying element to your Bass and Snare drum.

Advanced fills

In the Pop chapter I've covered some basic Fills that will help you transition between different sections of a song. As I've mentioned earlier, in Pop music, the instruments are more or less supposed to stay in the background. Now, Rock music is a different thing. It is perceived much more as a whole with all the involved instruments playing their respective roles. That allows us to get more creative with our drum parts. In fact, I want you to get creative now. Instead of just copying drum fills I've already programmed, I want you to come up with your own fills. How do you do that? Probably the easiest way is using a concept called *Linear Drumming*. What this means, is that only one element of the drum kit is played at a time. So whatever element you decide to use at any given time in the fill, it should be the only element that's played.

In order to get started, set your grid to 1/16 notes. How long you want your fill to be determines how many beats and hits you have to program. Your fill could be as short as just one beat (on the last beat of the last measure of a certain part of a song), or even spread over several measures. Since the principals stay the same no matter the fill-length you go for, we'll just work with fills that cover one measure here.

Once you have decided how long you want your fill to be, you need to decide which elements you want to use where. Basically, you can use all elements of the drum kit. However, I suggest focusing on the Snare and Bass drums, the Toms and Hi-hat. Use Crashes and the Ride cymbal sparingly. Just remember, only use one element at a time. A good tactic to get you started writing your fill is putting Snare drum hits on all the beats within the fill on the 1/16 notes grid.

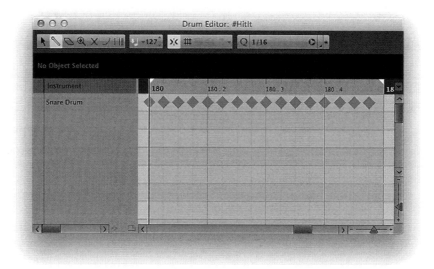

Figure 48: Grid: 1/16 notes, Appropriate tempo: Up to 180 BPM

You've probably noticed that this doesn't sound very distinct but kind of monotonous. So let's break it up a little.

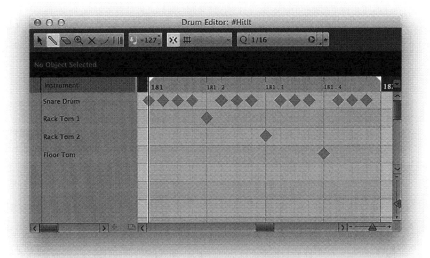

Figure 49: Grid: 1/16 notes, Appropriate tempo: Up to 180 BPM

That's already way better, don't you think? Let's add some more Toms.

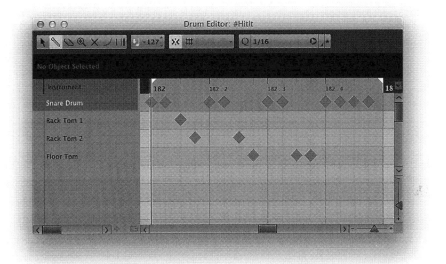

Figure 50: Grid: 1/16 notes, Appropriate tempo: Up to 180 BPM

Now we can also try to incorporate the Bass drum and the Hi-hat.

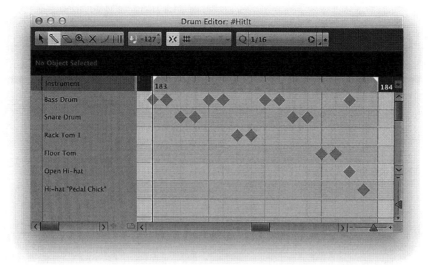

Figure 51: Grid: 1/16 notes, Appropriate tempo: Up to 180 BPM

The possibilities are nearly endless. Go crazy and try anything that comes to your mind. Four Snare drum hits at the beginning and at the end of the fill are a good starting point, but don't limit yourself to that. Use whatever you like, whatever feels and sounds right. Once you've got some good fills going, you don't even need to stop at the concept of linear drumming. Feel free to use more than one element at a time in your fills. The Bass drum, Snare drum, and Hi-Hat go particularly well together. Just remember to keep it realistic. Keep experimenting, and you will come up with more and more fills, one after another. Nevertheless, I'd like to show you a few fills that I have come up with as a starting point. Whether or not these are going to fit into your song highly depends on the mood and the tempo. Also "Less is more" in this case. I know I said we were free to actually play more stuff on the drums in Rock music than we were in Pop music, but that doesn't mean we have to force it. If it sounds good, it's fine. So without further ado, here are some advanced drum fills.

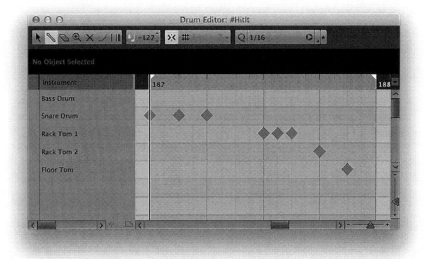

Figure 52: Grid: 1/16 notes, Appropriate tempo: 80-220 BPM

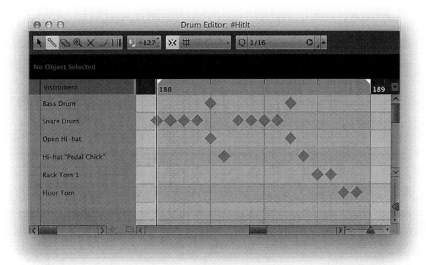

Figure 53: 1/16 notes, Appropriate tempo: 80-170 BPM

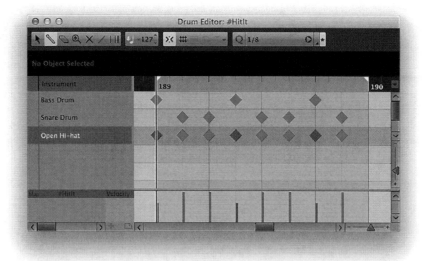

Figure 54: Grid: 1/8 notes, Appropriate tempo: 80-220 BPM

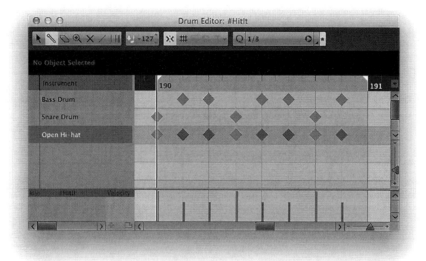

Figure 55: Grid: 1/8 notes, Appropriate tempo: 80-220 BPM

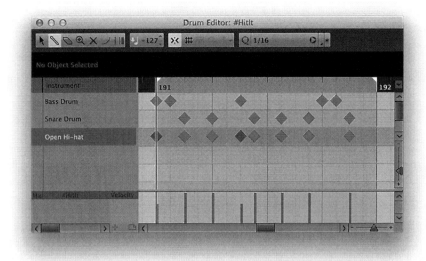

Figure 56: Grid: 1/16 notes, Appropriate tempo: 60-140 BPM

Pay special attention to the Hi-hat velocities on the last three fills. Since the Snare drum is the emphasized element in all of these, the Hi-hat accentuation tags along with it. Make sure to check out the Chapter on Humanization for more information about velocities, and how they affect the feel of fills and grooves.

Here are a few more traditional fills that I particularly like for their simplicity.

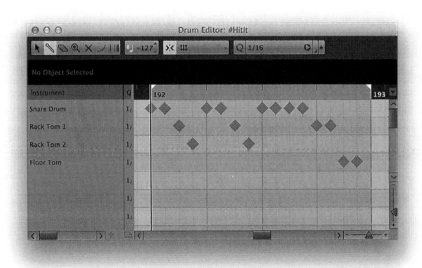

Figure 57: Grid: 1/16 notes, Appropriate tempo: 60-160 BPM

Here's a short one. In this example beats one and two in the measure represent the basic groove of the song whereas the fill takes up beats three and for.

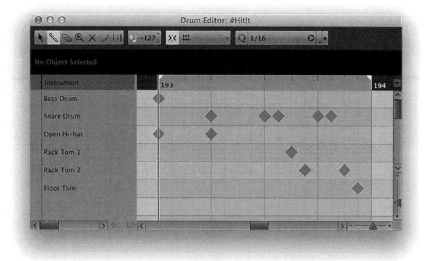

Figure 58: Grid: 1/16 notes, Appropriate tempo: 60-170 BPM

I've already mentioned this next fill in the Pop section, but it's one of my favorites, so it gets quite a lot of use across genres. Take this point into consideration here: don't be afraid to incorporate elements of other genres in your drum tracks. Like I said earlier, if it sound's good, it's fine. This is another short one so it only takes up beat four in the measure.

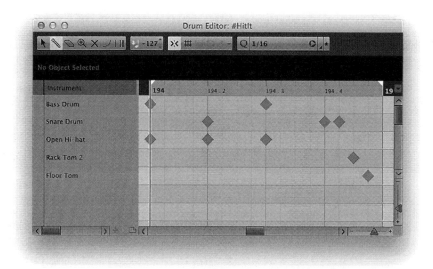

Figure 59: Grid: 1/16 notes, Appropriate tempo: 60-170 BPM

Triplet fills

We don't always have to use regular 1/16, 1/8, or 1/4 notes to create our grooves and fills. We can also use the respective triplet variants. Instead of two notes per beat (for 1/8 notes) or four notes per beat (for 1/16 notes), we get three notes per beat (with 1/8 triplets) or six notes per beat (with 1/16 triplets). Set your grid to 1/16 triplets, and try writing some fills using the principles presented above, only now make sure to use three (six) hits for every group of hits that used to be two (four) before. If you want to use 1/8 triplets, just leave every second spot on the grid blank (or set it to 1/8 triplets in the first place for further convenience). You'll immediately notice how the feel of the fills changes drastically.

You can also combine triplets and regular notes. In the following fill the first two beats consist of six 1/8 triplets and the rest is 1/16 notes. Note that you will have to change your grid settings during the writing process to be able to do that.

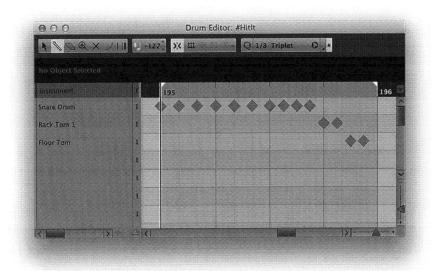

Figure 60: Grid: 1/8 notes triplets, 1/16 notes, Appropriate tempo: 60-160 BPM

Triplets are also a great way to transition between tempos. For example, if the next part is played in half time a triplet fill can make the transition sound more natural. Again, in the following example only the last to beats of the measure make up the fill, whereas the rest represents the basic groove of the song.

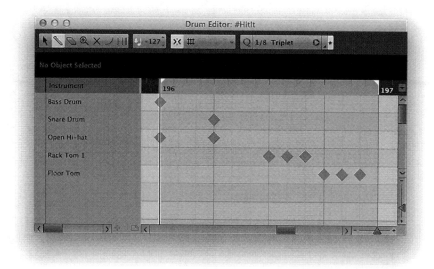

Figure 61: Grid: 1/8 notes triplets, Appropriate tempo: 90-220 BPM

Try playing with triplets a little more before you move on to the next chapter. We are going to use them quite a bit in the upcoming Metal section of this book.

Ending fills

Since we use fills to transition between parts of a song (or to break up the rhythm within the same section of a song), the next measure after the fill usually needs to be emphasized somehow. We can easily do that using Crashes and the Bass drum. Both are often played at the same time for added impact. Since the Bass drum is played with the foot and the drummer has two hands, you can even use both Crash cymbals and the Bass drum at the same time. So basically all you have to do is exchange the first hit of your main groove with the Crash/Bass drum combination and keep going as usual. Let's say the following example is a (simple) main groove of a song.

Figure 62: Simple groove

If this groove were to follow a fill, it could be changed to the following in order to emphasize the new section of the song.

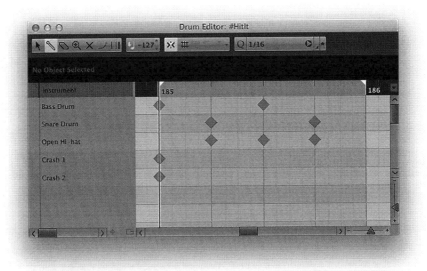

Figure 63: Simple groove following a fill (not shown)

Another interesting alternative is to place a Crash cymbal on beat two together with the Snare drum instead of on beat one. You can often hear this on *Metallica* songs, for example.

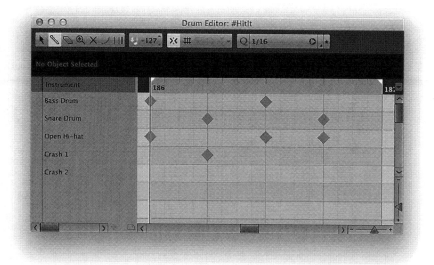

Figure 64: Simple groove following a fill (variation)

If you decide to go for that variant, make sure to only use one Crash cymbal, since you are using the Snare drum at the same time (which is played with one of the Drummer's two hands).

In the following chapter you'll wish Drummers actually had five hands and three feet because it's time for some Metal and we could definitely make use of as many limbs as we can get.

Metal

If you've never written or listened to Metal music, there is one thing you need to know: Metal by itself is larger than life. And so is everything that goes along with it. That includes drum tracks. Play *fast* and hit *hard*. As you might expect, this is quite an exaggeration, but there are some takeaway points here: in no other genre can we make use of as many elements of the drum kit as in Metal. Furthermore, we don't have to stay in the background anymore. In fact the drums take on a very prominent role.

If you've read the section on locking-in your Drum tracks with the rest of the music in any given song, you have a great starting point for writing Metal drum tracks. Do this as much as you can, and you will immediately knock out great results. Because guitar riffs are usually more complex in Metal than in other genres, they provide a solid foundation for your bass and snare drum combinations. There is a guitar playing technique called "palm muting" that's very popular among Metal guitar players. Move on to the next paragraph to find out how you can use it to improve your drum tracks.

Locking-in with palm muting

When a Metal guitar player hits the strings of his instrument with his picking hand, what you'll hear most of the time is a loud, distorted, aggressive, and certainly very open, sustaining sound. However, if he uses the palm muting technique, he will put the side of his picking hand on the strings while he picks them. The result is a percussive, choppy, somewhat "chunky", and considerably shorter sound. If you listen closely to your favorite Metal tunes, you will easily spot the parts where this technique is used. Metal guitar players will often use Palm muting, quickly alternating with picking the strings regularly. Due to the speed of Metal music, picking techniques can change from one 1/16 note (or sometimes even 1/32 note) to the next. We can use this extreme and constant variation to our advantage.

Remember what I have written about how to build the most basic groove? Simply place the Bass drum on beats one and three, and the Snare drum on beats two and four. This is also our starting point for this writing technique. Now, let's build on that. Place additional Bass drum hits wherever there is a palm muted note in the underlying guitar riff, except on beats two and four. These are still reserved for the Snare drum. However it's fine to place Bass drum hits on the 1/16 or 1/32 notes directly before or after the Snare drum hits. There is one exception to this rule and that's when a palm muting patterns uses 1/16 or 1/32 notes that extend across beat(s) two and/or four. In this case don't omit the Bass drum on beat(s) two and/or four. Just add it along with the Snare drum. You'll notice that in many of the examples below. Remember:

1. Metal playing can be extremely fast at times and the palm muted notes of a certain guitar riff can have note values of 1/16 or sometimes even 1/32.

2. Don't put any drum hit wherever there is no accentuated note (through palm muting or otherwise) in the guitar riff (apart from the aforementioned Snare drum hits on beats two and four).

3. Last but not least, add the accompanying element of your choice (Hi-hat, Ride, or in the case of Metal – even Crash cymbals) with appropriate note values (1/4 and 1/8 notes will work best most of the time).

And there you have it. You've just successfully locked-in your Bass drum and Snare drum hits with the palm muting going on in the guitar riffs of your song. This should easily get you off the ground when trying to come up with great Metal drum tracks.

Another no-brainer in Metal is using Double Bass drum beats. They will be the topic of the next section.

Double Bass drum beats

Double Bass drum beats have been a constant in Metal music since the early 80s. Ever since their introduction, their heavy pounding and driving force has struck fear into the heart of non-believers.

That might be a bit of an exaggeration right there. But in all seriousness, double Bass drum beats play a major role in Metal drumming. Fortunately, they are really easy to program. Given their impact, you might almost feel ashamed at how easily you can get a professional sounding groove going.

Here's how you do it. First, place a Snare drum hit on beats two and four. Now set your grid to 1/16 notes if you haven't done so already, and place a Bass drum hit on every single 1/16 note in the measure. Add the accompanying element of your choice (Hi-hat, Ride, or Crash cymbal) on every 1/4 or 1/8 note and you're done. Here is what it should look like.

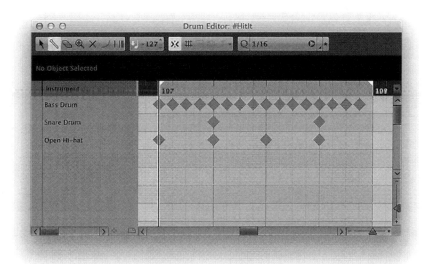

Figure 65: Grid: 1/16 notes, Appropriate tempo: 80-220 BPM

This also works with 1/16 notes triples.

Figure 66: Grid: 1/16 notes triplets, Appropriate tempo: 75-190 BPM

For faster tempos, where the 1/16 triplet variant would sound ridiculous, you can use 1/8 notes triplets.

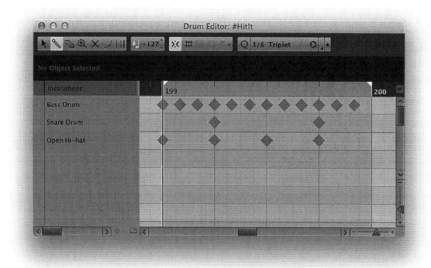

Figure 67: Grid: 1/8 notes triplets, Appropriate tempo: 60-240 BPM

Like on previous occasions, you are free to add additional Snare drum hits to make the rhythm more interesting.

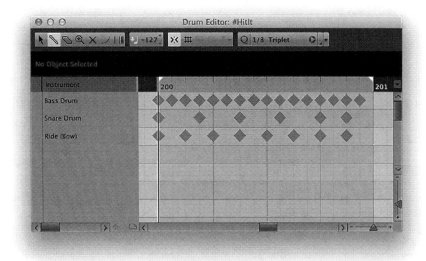

Figure 68: Grid: 1/16 notes, Appropriate tempo: 75-150 BPM

This is just one example of many. Get creative and try out different variations. Also, keep this approach in mind whenever you need to incorporate accents corresponding to the guitar, bass, or vocal riff in your drum tracks. Just put a Snare snare drum hit wherever the accents are.

You can also break it up a little, and don't use the Bass drum all the way through the pattern. In order to keep it powerful, I've used bursts of 1/32 notes on the Bass drum in the following example.

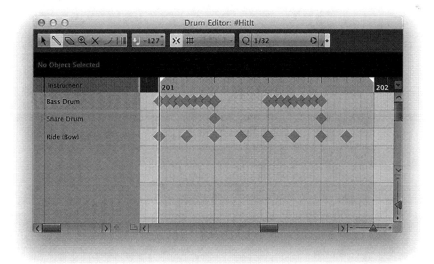

Figure 69: Grid: 1/32 notes, Appropriate tempo: 60-150 BPM

Here's a variation of the above groove with 1/16 notes triplets.

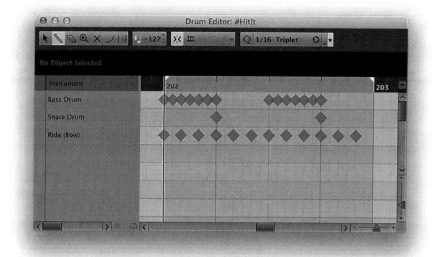

Figure 70: Grid: 1/16 notes triplets, Appropriate tempo: 50-170 BPM

If these Bass drum bursts are not what your song needs, try groups of four to eight 1/16 note Bass drum hits and experiment with their position within the measure. Here are a few examples.

Figure 71: Grid: 1/16 notes, Appropriate tempo: 60-210 BPM

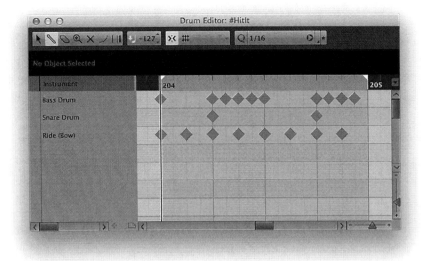

Figure 72: Grid: 1/16 notes, Appropriate tempo: 60-210 BPM

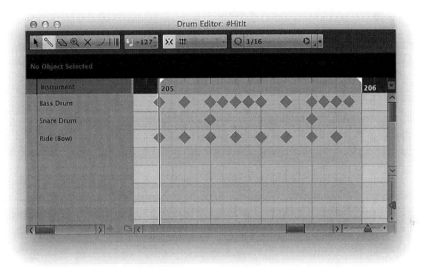

Figure 73: Grid: 1/16 notes, Appropriate tempo: 60-210 BPM

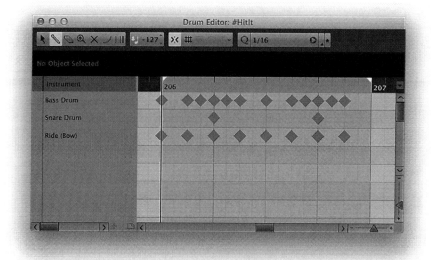

Figure 74: Grid: 1/16 notes, Appropriate tempo: 60-210 BPM

Alternatively, fast bursts and slower double Bass drum patterns can be combined. While the possibilities are once again endless, here is an example.

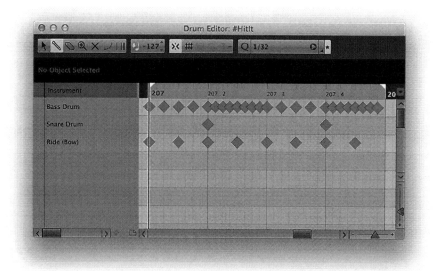

Figure 75: Grid: 1/32 notes, Appropriate tempo: 60-130 BPM

Needless to say, you don't have to stick with your Snare drum on beats two and four only. Go back to the Rock chapter and check out the section about Snare drum comping again. Apply it to your Metal tracks in combination with the double Bass drum beats from above to get even more interesting grooves.

A more classic kind of groove that you'll find in a lot of older and more melodic songs is the "Gallop groove". It got its name from the sound that horses make when galloping across an open field. As soon as you program it for yourself, you will notice the resemblance. Even though it's not a full-on double Bass drum beat, it still involves a double Bass drum pattern. This one is sometimes wrongly called a "Triplet groove", because there are three consecutive Bass drum hits played quickly after another. However, they are straight 1/16 notes and not triplets as you can see in the next example.

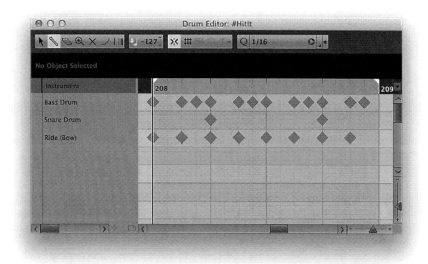

Figure 76: Grid: 1/16 notes, Appropriate tempo: 120-190 BPM

This next one is a variation of the classic Gallop groove that is nowadays used in a lot of Metalcore and Melodic Death Metal types of music. It sounds best at high tempos.

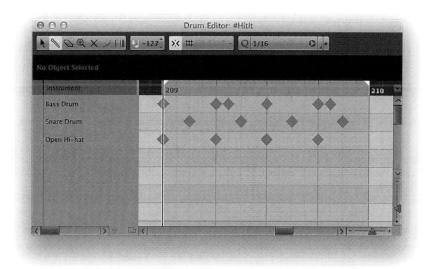

Figure 77: Grid: 1/16 notes, Appropriate tempo: 110-240 BPM

If you need to take it even further than these double Bass drum beats, you should definitely look into Blast beats.

Blast beats

Blast beats are probably the most powerful kind of beats out there. Originating from subgenres like Death and Black Metal, they are now much more common in the more melodic variants of Metal. There are a number of different Blast beats out there, so we will go over each one of them.

The *Traditional Blast* involves alternating Bass drum and Snare drum hits using 1/16 notes. Furthermore, there is an accompanying element of your choice (Hi-hat or Ride or Crash cymbal or China) on the same hits as the Bass drum.

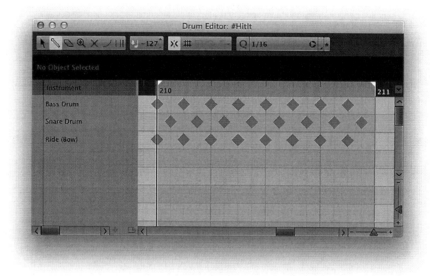

Figure 78: Grid: 1/16 notes, Appropriate tempo: 80-200 BPM

Of course you can also use 1/16 notes triplets to program it in a triplet feel, if that suits your song better.

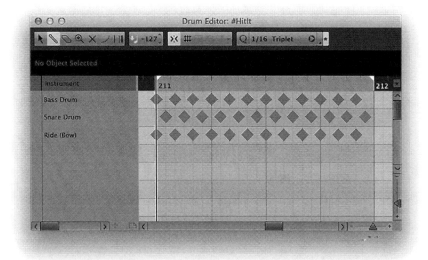

Figure 79: Grid: 1/16 notes triplets, Appropriate tempo: 60-160 BPM

As you may have noticed, the Bass drum is leading this groove, but you can also turn that around, both in a regular and a triplet feel.

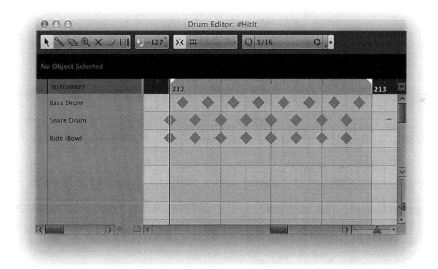

Figure 80: Grid: 1/16 notes, Appropriate tempo: 80-200 BPM

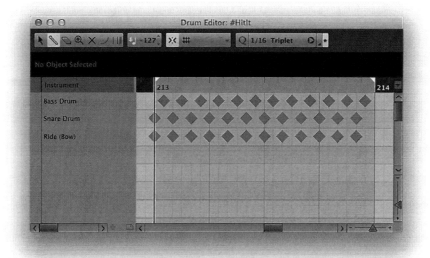

Figure 81: Grid: 1/16 notes triplets, Appropriate tempo: 60-160 BPM

The *Hammer Blast* might be the simplest of all the Blast beats. It consists only of 1/16 notes on the Bass and Snare drum, with the accompanying element of your choice. If the Hammer Blast is played at very high tempos, it's called a *Hyper Blast*.

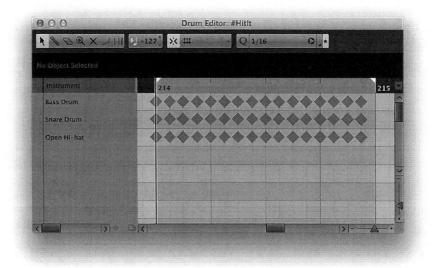

Figure 82: Grid: 1/16 notes, Appropriate tempo: 85-150 BPM

Here it is in a triplet feel using 1/8 notes triplets.

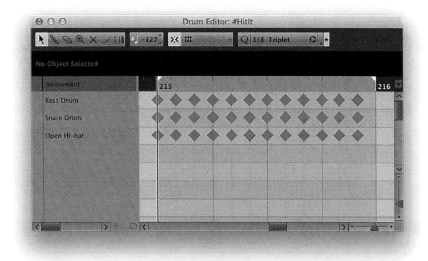

Figure 83: Grid: 1/8 notes triplets, Appropriate tempo: 100-180 BPM

The *Bomb Blast* is essentially a double Bass drum beat with 1/8 notes Snare drum hits on top of it and the accompanying element of your choice tagging along with it.

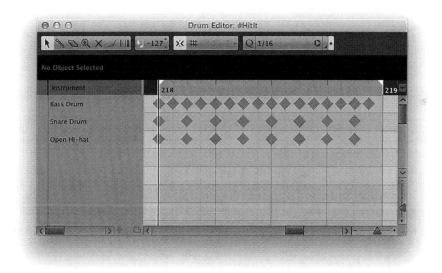

Figure 84: Grid: 1/16 notes, Appropriate tempo: 110-180 BPM

In a triplet feel it looks like this.

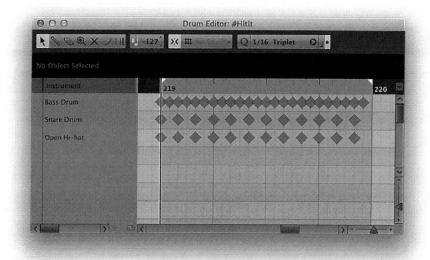

Figure 85: Grid: 1/8 notes triplets, Appropriate tempo: 105-135 BPM

If you turn it around and let the Bass drum lead you should end up with something closely resembling the following two examples (for a regular and a triplet feel respectively).

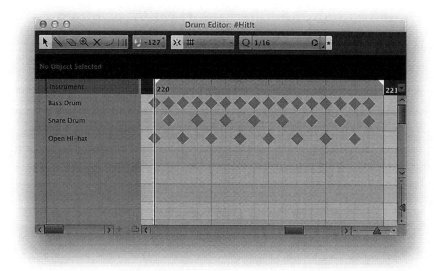

Figure 86: Grid: 1/16 notes, Appropriate tempo: 110-180 BPM

Figure 87: Grid: 1/8 notes triplets, Appropriate tempo: 105-135 BPM

The *Gravity Blast* is centered on the Snare drum, which plays 1/16 notes all the way through while the Bass drum and the accompanying element come in every other hit. It is also known as *Freehand Blast* and works both in a regular and triplet feel.

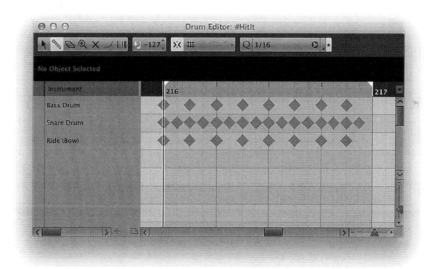

Figure 88: Grid: 1/16 notes, Appropriate tempo: 90-160 BPM

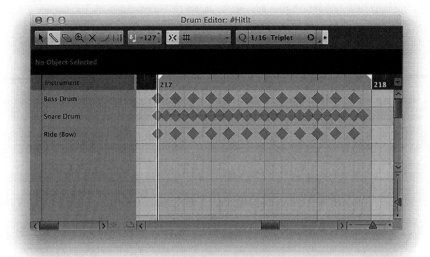

Figure 89: Grid: 1/16 notes triplets, Appropriate tempo: 70-110 BPM

The *Skank beat* is very similar to the traditional Blast, but it comes with an accompanying element on every hit instead of only on the on-beats, like in the traditional Blast.

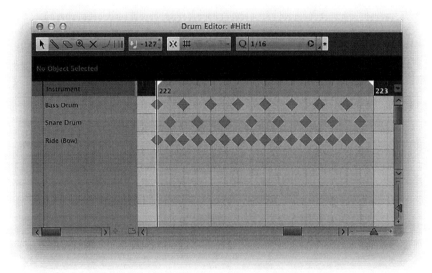

Figure 90: Grid: 1/16 notes, Appropriate tempo: 90-140 BPM

It also works in a triplet feel.

Figure 91: Grid: 1/16 notes triplets, Appropriate tempo: 80-125 BPM

Of course, the Snare can lead as well.

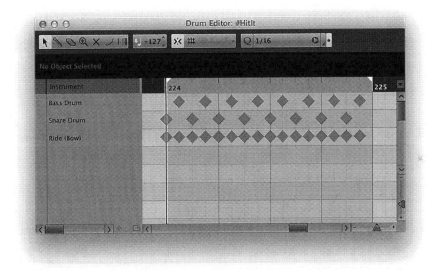

Figure 92: Grid: 1/16 notes, Appropriate tempo: 90-140 BPM

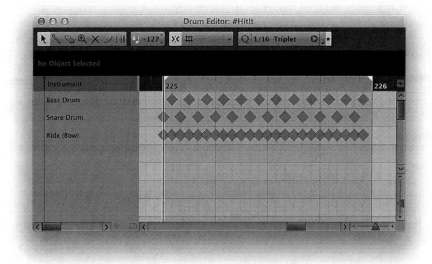

Figure 93: Grid: 1/16 notes triplets, Appropriate tempo: 80-125 BPM

Especially when played at very fast tempos, Blast beats can sound somewhat robotic. Make sure to check out the chapter on velocities to find out how to prevent that.

Since it's physically impossible for a real drummer to play a Blast beat for a very long time, we need to consider that fact in our programming. We need to break up a Blast beat every now and then, or transition to another kind of beat. This is exactly what the fills that are discussed in the next sections are used for.

Basic Metal fills

As mentioned earlier, drums take up a more prominent role in Metal than in some of the other genres of music. For this reason, fills also become more sophisticated. Still, some of the stuff that's featured on the following pages might just as well be an advanced Rock fill. Let's start it off with an easy variant, just two groups of four on the Floor Tom, and the Base drum.

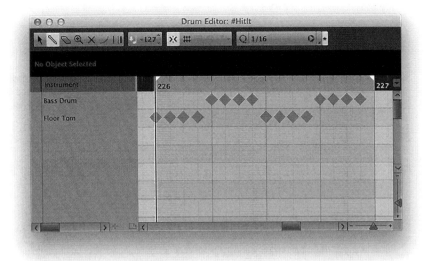

Figure 94: Grid: 1/16 notes, Appropriate tempo: 90-180 BPM

Groups of four can also be played in 1/32 notes.

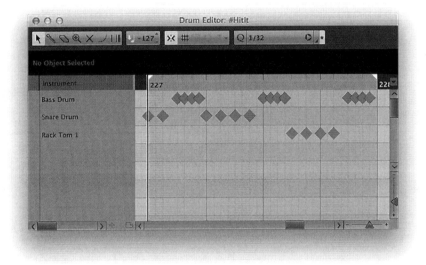

Figure 95: Grid: 1/32 notes, Appropriate tempo: 95-135 BPM

Here's another one involving groups of four, but this time all the Toms are used.

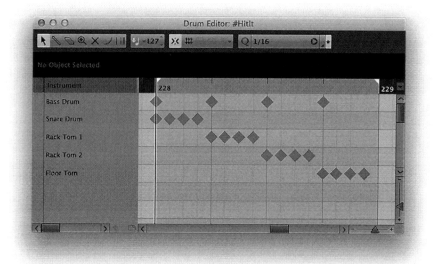

Figure 96: Grid: 1/16 notes, Appropriate tempo: 85-180 BPM

You can break it up even further and use groups of two.

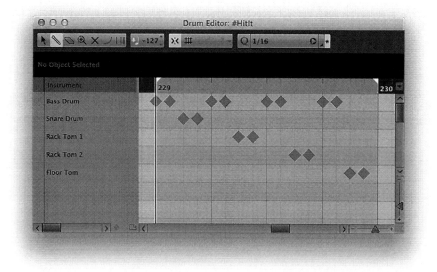

Figure 97: Grid: 1/16 notes, Appropriate tempo: 85-180 BPM

While the last fill started off every beat with the Bass drum, this next one is exactly the other way around.

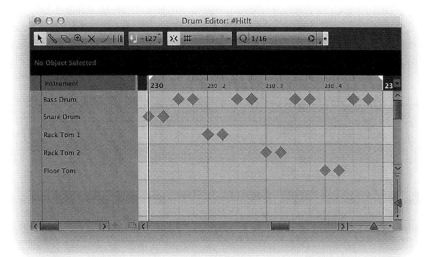

Figure 98: Grid: 1/16 notes, Appropriate tempo: 85-180 BPM

You don't always have to work your way down through all the Toms, as this next fill illustrates.

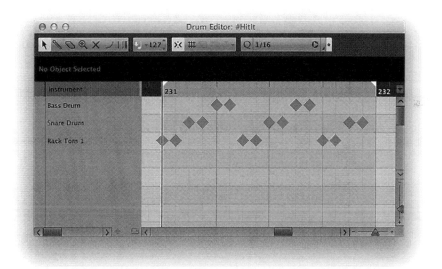

Figure 99: Grid: 1/16 notes, Appropriate tempo: 85-180 BPM

Here's a variant that includes three Toms and could also be used (in part) as a Tom-centered rhythm groove.

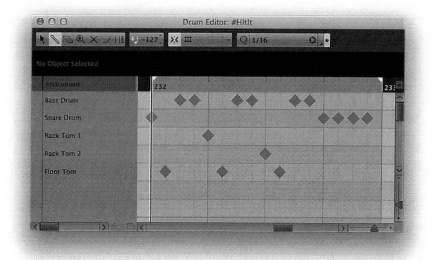

Figure 100: Grid: 1/16 notes, Appropriate tempo: 100-170 BPM

This next one is also Tom heavy.

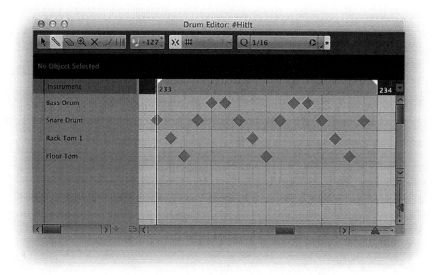

Figure 101: Grid: 1/16 notes, Appropriate tempo: 110-170 BPM

In this example, the Snare drum is fairly constant, while the fill works its way down through all the Toms.

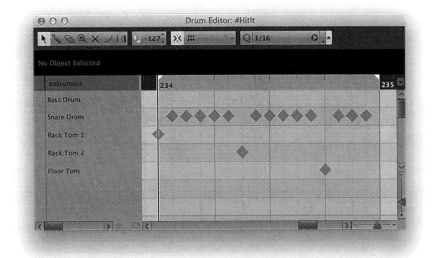

Figure 102: Grid: 1/16 notes, Appropriate tempo: 85-125 BPM

While involving a Tom, this next one is still pretty much centered on the Snare drum.

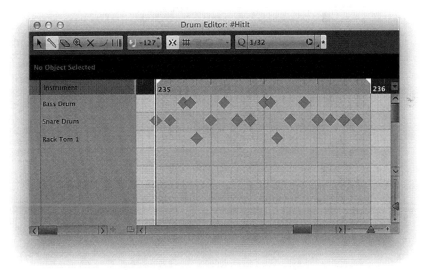

Figure 103: Grid: 1/32 notes, Appropriate tempo: 85-110 BPM

There are endless ways in which we could incorporate a downward descent on the Toms. Here's another one.

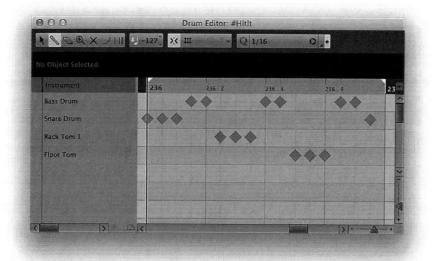

Figure 104: Grid: 1/16 notes, Appropriate tempo: 110-170 BPM

This next fill is based on 1/16 notes triplets, and even involves a flam (Turn of the grid and put a second Snare drum hit closely in front of the one directly on beat three to program that.).

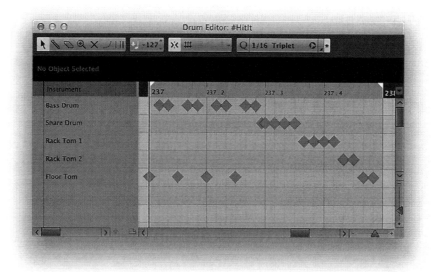

Figure 105: Grid: 1/16 notes triplets, Appropriate tempo: 80-120 BPM

Whether or not this next one will work within your song, really depends on what the other instruments are playing.

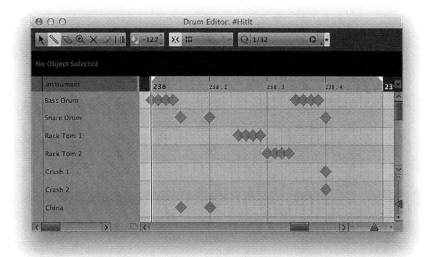

Figure 106: Grid: 1/32 notes, Appropriate tempo: 90-120 BPM

The two hits on the Snare drum (supported by the China) as well as the two Crashes in the end will attract a lot of attention, so make sure that they go well with the other elements in the arrangement. Alternatively, you can rearrange the fill to fit your needs.

The next fill is similar to the first one in this section, although based on 1/32 notes, and therefore twice as fast. This works particularly well to break up a monotonous fast part, for example, in the middle of a double Bass drum driven verse.

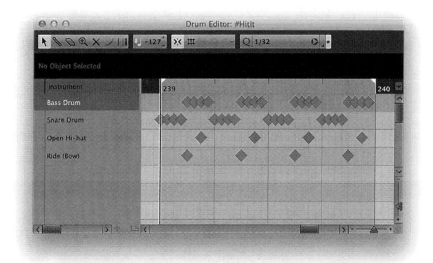

Figure 107: Grid: 1/32 notes, Appropriate tempo: 80-100 BPM

To finish off this section here are three Tom heavy fills.

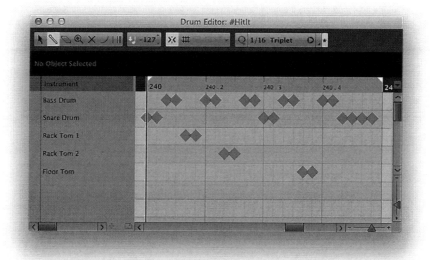

Figure 108: Grid: 1/16 notes triplets, Appropriate tempo: 80-130 BPM

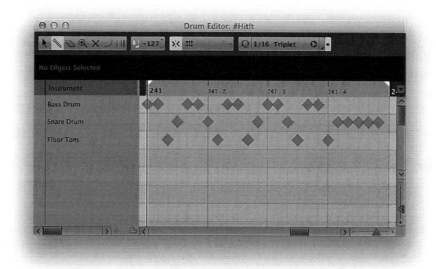

Figure 109: Grid: 1/16 notes triplets, Appropriate tempo: 80-120 BPM

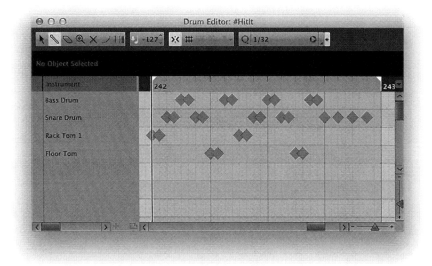

Figure 110: Grid: 1/32 notes, Appropriate tempo: 60-100 BPM

Remember, if the tempo of some of these fills doesn't seem to fit the song that you are working on, you can always double the note values (for example use 1/16 notes instead of 1/32 notes) and spread them out over two measures or cut the note values in half effectively reducing the fill to two beats.

Advanced Metal fills

Metal is somewhat of an over-the-top kind of genre. Therefore, it seems only logical that we need more complex fills to suit. Therefore some of these span across two measures. As you will notice, it's also more common to incorporate cymbals like the Hi-hat, Ride, China, or Crash in the middle of fills. Feel free to exchange any of the contained cymbals for others you might like better.

The first fill might seem fairly basic, except for the China.

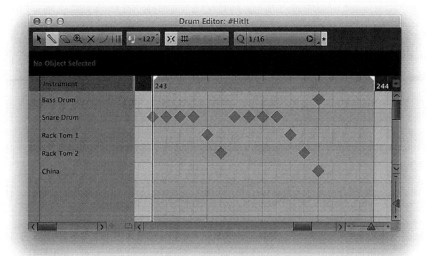

Figure 111: Grid: 1/16 notes, Appropriate tempo: 100-150 BPM

This one spans across two measures and revolves around alternating Snare drum and Bass drum hits with the occasional Tom thrown in.

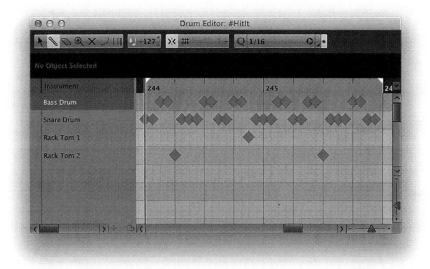

Figure 112: Grid: 1/16 notes, Appropriate tempo: 95-160 BPM

Here is another one involving the China, or any other cymbal you choose to put down.

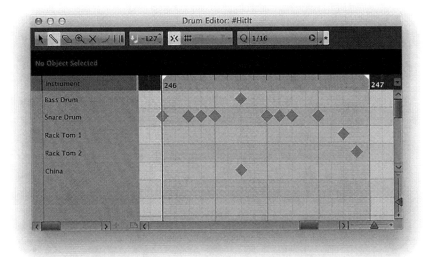

Figure 113: Grid: 1/16 notes, Appropriate tempo: 125-180 BPM

In this fill, the Ride cymbal is used almost like an additional drum. You can try and exchange it for any of the Toms to get a more traditional feel.

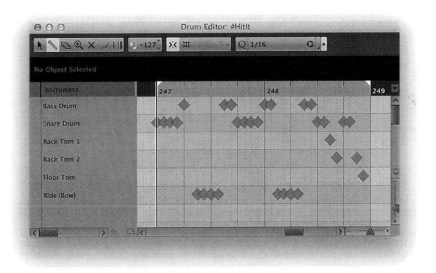

Figure 114: Grid: 1/16 notes, Appropriate tempo: 120-170 BPM

I've found Hi-hat barking to be ideally suited to lead up to new song sections. Check out the following example to get the idea.

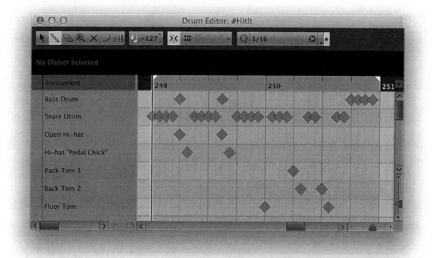

Figure 115: Grid: 1/16 notes, Appropriate tempo: 100-160 BPM

Here's another Tom heavy fill.

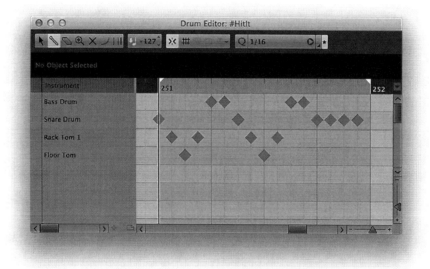

Figure 116: Grid: 1/16 notes, Appropriate tempo: 100-160 BPM

In Metal, the triplet feel plays a large role for fills, so here are three fills as a starting point for you.

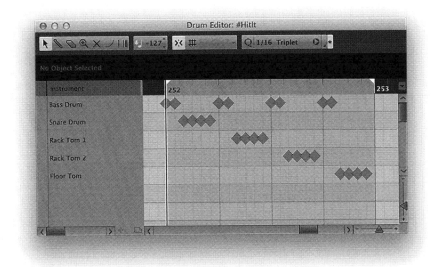

Figure 117: Grid: 1/16 notes triplets, Appropriate tempo: 90-140 BPM

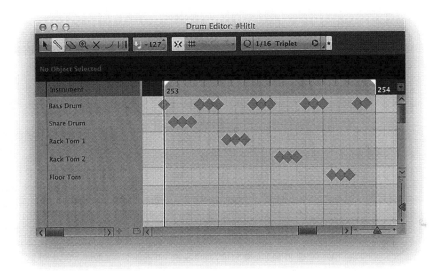

Figure 118: Grid: 1/16 notes triplets, Appropriate tempo: 90-140 BPM

Notice how these two each have their own distinctive feel? Even though they look similar the combination of four Tom and two Bass drum hits in the first fill sounds quite different from the three Tom and three Bass drum hits in the second one.

The last one of these is one of my personal favorites.

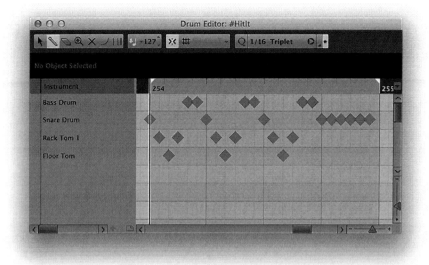

Figure 119: Grid: 1/16 notes triplets, Appropriate tempo: 90-140 BPM

While fills are great for transitioning between song parts and breaking up otherwise monotonous passages, they are not the only way to spice up your drum tracks.

Accompanying element variations

If you are working with a straightforward double Bass drum beat or an otherwise rather simple beat, it might be a good idea to try to vary the accompanying element. Instead of a simple 1/4 or 1/8 note rhythm you can add in a completely different rhythm. This can either be locked-in with any other element in the arrangement or, if the arrangement is rather monotonous itself, you can create a completely independent rhythm. Whether any given rhythm will fit what you are doing or not highly depends on your song. So, you have to listen closely and decide for yourself how much you want to stray from the path. To give you an idea of what kind of feel can be achieved with this technique, here are two examples.

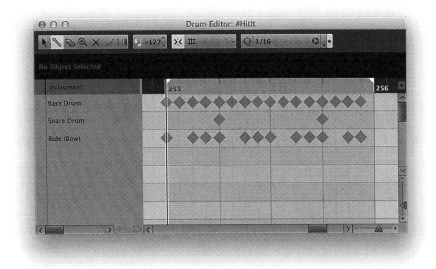

Figure 120: Grid: 1/16 notes, Appropriate tempo: 75-180 BPM

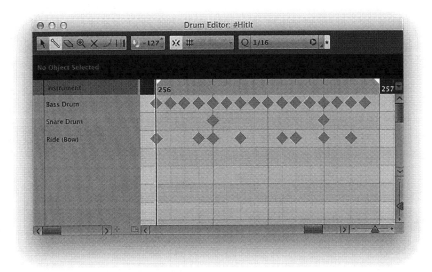

Figure 121: Grid: 1/16 notes, Appropriate tempo: 100-160 BPM

To achieve yet another completely different feel, you can use the Crash cymbals as explained in the following section.

The Crash cymbals

So far we've mainly used the Crash cymbals as a means to start of a new part of a song and to put certain accents here and there. However, in Metal, we can make even more use of them and use them as an accompanying element just like we would use the Hi-hat or Ride cymbal. Using Crash cymbals this way really conveys a sense of power and a forward-drive that's not present in other styles of music. They can also make slow parts appear incredibly heavy.

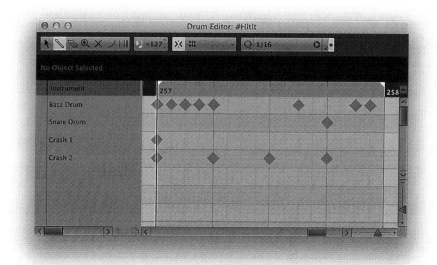

Figure 122: Grid: 1/16 notes, Appropriate tempo: 90-110 BPM

So, whenever you feel a certain part needs a little bit more power, try using a Crash cymbal instead of the Hi-hat or Ride.

Humanizing beats

When programming drums, the biggest challenge apart from coming up with the actual beats, is making the programmed tracks sound natural. In general, only few people enjoy listening to a drum track that's all robotic and easily spotted as programmed right away, unless it's for specific effect. So, it's our job to make our beats seem as "human" as possible.

Whether or not this is a difficult task depends on the genre we are working in. In modern Pop music, a large amount of drum tracks are actually programmed. As a result, it's easier to create professional sounding tracks. It's similar in Metal. While the majority of Metal tracks are recorded using live drums, they are later edited to perfection, making them sound almost machine-like at times. There is an ongoing discussion in the producer community, as to whether or not Metal drums should sound less perfect, and more natural instead. Luckily, we can use the current trend to our advantage and create great Metal drums comparatively easy. The most difficult genre to get right is probably Rock. Depending on how you define Rock, it might involve a lot of band-oriented music, where all the musicians and their respective instruments work together to create the groove. This is where you might have to pay attention to the most nuances.

In order to achieve the realistic sound we are looking for, we basically have two parameters on our hands: *Quantization* and *Velocity*. Quantization takes care of how close to the grid each hit is positioned, while the velocity of each hit defines how hard the virtual drum or cymbal is hit, hence how loud it is. In the forthcoming sections, we will go over how we can alter these two in order to get the desired result.

Quantization

As technology evolved over the last 15 to 25 years or so, music production has partly become more of a technical process than an artistic one. Studio equipment and software became more advanced, with musicians and producers using what was available to them to refine their tracks as best as they could. Of course, playing techniques have also evolved. As a result, music fans have grown accustomed to a very "tight" sound over time. Nonetheless, even the best drummers in the world are never one hundred percent "on time". They will always be a few milliseconds late or early, and that's the difference between humans and drum machines.

When programming drums in the real world, we have to use the grid. If we were to just put all the drum hits in without any point of visual reference, it wouldn't work. So while you are writing your grooves, just work with the grid. When you are finished programming all the drums for your track you can start worrying about quantization – or undoing it, I should say.

Luckily, this isn't as much work as you would expect. Most recording software offers some kind of setting for how far off the grid hits should be played. This differs a little from software to software but look out for settings called "Humanize", "Humanization", "Random", "Randomization", "Swing" or similar. You'll most likely find them somewhere around the MIDI settings, the Quantization settings, or the Grid settings of your DAW. Please consult your software's manual if you can't find it right away. Once you have found the setting, we need to figure out how to adjust it for the desired effect.

Experience shows that different DAWs handle their parameters in their own ways, so the best way to set this up is not by some preset, but by ear. Here's what you need to listen out for. Make sure the setting (whatever it may be called in your software) is turned on, but its parameter is turned all the way down to the lowest possible value. Now, while playing back one of your drum tracks, bring it all the way up. Your drums should be all over the place immediately. Slowly turn it back down until it's not so crazy anymore, and it feels normal to you again. And that's it! Turn the setting on and off with the parameter left unaltered. You should hear the difference easily. With the Humanize setting turned off, the drums will most likely feel somewhat uncomfortable to you now.

By the way, the best way to perform the adjustment is with your eyes closed, so that you are not influenced by what you can see onscreen.

Depending on your DAW, there might be additional parameters to further fine-tune these intended inaccuracies. If your software doesn't have these extra parameters, I'll show you how to work around that. Basically there are three different ways a real drummer would play (either on purpose or subconscious), and we can aim our off-the-grid hits in the same direction to get specific results.

1. **Early**: This can be a great option to spice up your heavier tracks. Instead of right on the beat, the drummer hits just a little before the click. This makes for a great forward drive and can really give a new perspective when limited to a certain section of a song, for example, the verse or the chorus. Work with the underlying music and sometimes even the lyrics to get a feel whether or not this technique is appropriate in your particular application. Ask yourself: Are there any words that call for action, some kind of forward motion, anything positive or aggressive? You can also use this in combination with bringing the tempo up a few BPM.

2. **Late**: Being the opposite of early this can help you to kick back the groove of the song for a more laid back feel. You can use this in the verse as a counterpart to a heavy chorus, or maybe in the bridge to slow things down a bit. This might also be a good fit for quiet ballads. Also, try bringing the tempo down a few BPM on the parts that are played with a laid back feel.

3. **Regular**: I called the third option "Regular" for lack of a better word. However, what I mean by it, is no special emphasize on early or late hits

but rather little variations in both ways. This is what closest resembles a drummer that's playing to the beat to the best of his ability. This will most likely be the way to go for the majority of occasions.

How you can get this set up depends on your DAW. If you have just a general "humanize" or similar control, this will be the setting you need to adjust to get the "regular" scenario going, meaning this will cause early as well as late hits.

Other software might give you more control as to whether hits are early or late, as well as separate controls for the maximum offset before and after the grid. In case of that scenario, all you have to do if you go either for an early or a late feel is turn up the respective control to your liking, and leave the other one unaltered.

If you have only one control, you are a little limited when it comes to setting up natural sounding variations, but you can still get good results using the following method. Program your drums with the grid turned on just like you normally would. Once you are finished with the whole track, turn off the grid and hit "Select All" on your drum track. Carefully move everything a little bit forward or backward (depending on whether you want an early or a late feel) by hand until it sounds right. Now your groove is off the grid, but it's still static. Start turning up your "Humanize" control to get rid of that. Since you dragged everything away from the grid manually already this will most likely cause hits that are too far out. In order to fix that move all the hits back in just a little bit. In addition to that you can also turn the general "Humanize" control back down a little. And there you have it.

Of course, you can always freely move around individual hits in addition to all of the above. If you take this to the extreme, you could manually adjust every hit on its own. Ultimately this will give you the best results. However, I think in terms of efficiency, the method I described earlier can't be beat. Therefore, I would recommend it as a starting point, and go in to edit individual hits at key points in the song. For example, if the underlying music calls for an early or late Snare hit here and there.

As mentioned earlier, I also recommend using the tempo of your song as a means of enhancing the groove. Turning it up or down by just two to four BPM in certain parts of the song can make a huge difference. However, that's only possible if you don't program your drums to pre-recorded music, or if the music only consist of scratch tracks that will be re-recorded once you perfect the drum track. Otherwise, the two won't fit together if you start altering the tempo of the drums without altering the tempo of the rest of the music. Whether or not varying the tempo of your song is appropriate or not (and if so in which parts of the song) is highly subjective, so the best way to figure out the right option is by experimenting.

Velocities

We've already touched on velocities in one of the earlier chapters in order for a "build-up" fill to work. However, this was just a brief introduction to velocities and we will discuss them in detail in this section.

As I've stated before, velocities determine how hard virtual drums and cymbals are hit. The harder they are hit, the louder the sound of the drum or cymbal. More importantly the characteristics of a drum or cymbal sound changes with the velocity. For example, a Snare drum or cymbal will have much more attack if it's hit really hard.

Note: The velocity of any given hit can have any value from 0 to 127 (128 different values in total), the latter being the loudest. While some DAWs might range from 0 to 100 (101 different values) instead the MIDI in the background still ranges from 0 to 127. So a regular MIDI value of 100 would compare to 79 in one such DAW (100 / 128 x 101) whereas a velocity value of 90 in a DAW that's set up to range from 0 to 100 would compare to 114 in regular MIDI (90 / 101 x 128).

Finding the right velocity for the right occasion is the real challenge here. For that I've come up with a set of certain velocity values that I use as a starting point to achieve a certain loudness and/or sound characteristic. In addition to that, I will you use another humanization feature build into most DAWs. But first of all, here are the Velocity values I use:

15, 31, 47, 63, 79, 95, 111, 127

It's important to note that different drum software react differently to velocity values. While some will have a lot of velocity layers and play a different sound as soon as you change the velocity value by a few steps, others might already play back the their loudest sound if the Velocity is set to 100. It's almost impossible to develop a set of values that will work with ever piece of software alike, especially since there are more and more expansion add-ons released frequently. Therefore, it's very important that you choose the drum software you want to use for a particular song before you start working on velocities. Otherwise, you might have to go over the velocities again after changing the drum software used. The above set worked well on all the different software platforms I've used so far. Ultimately it doesn't matter if you use these values, or if you find others that work better for you. If you find other values to work better with your specific drum software, don't hesitate to use them instead. For any application I describe below, just substitute your personal values if you like.

The first value I'd like to discuss is *111*. This is my go-to velocity value for Pop and softer Rock stuff. So what this means is, whenever I'm programming something in the vain of said genres, I will set the velocity to 111, which results in every hit I put down on the grid being played back at 111 automatically. For me, this seems to be the ideal velocity for this occasion most of the time. The idea behind it, is that a drummer performing this kind of music will hit hard and consistently but not the hardest he possibly can. Keep that in mind when using this velocity, certain elements of the drum kit might seem louder than others because their sound character simply has more presence. Don't be afraid to use your drum software's mixer to make up for that. See the bonus chapter on mixing for additional tips and tricks.

127 is my "full-on" value. I use this for heavy Rock as well as Metal stuff. If you watch drummers play these genres, you will notice how they give it all they've got, often sweating wildly and leaving the stage exhausted after a show. So that's why I set the velocity to 127 when programming drums for this type of music.

Surprisingly, these two values tend to be the ones I use most often. All the others are just complementary values that I use to liven up the groove.

If you listen to a professional drum track recorded with live drums, you will notice that even though drummers generally play very consistent at the "live equivalent" of 111 or 127, they throw in weaker hits here and there. Part of that might be intentional, while part of it happens more subconsciously. It is our job to mimic this behavior as best as possible, in order to achieve a realistic and natural sound. Let's talk about how we can achieve that for the actual drums first.

The way I start out optimizing drum tracks velocity-wise, is by looking at sequences of the same drum being hit multiple times in a row. For example, this could be two consecutive 1/8 Bass drum notes, a Tom fill, a Snare drum roll, or even a double Bass part. In my experience, the first note in such a sequence is always the loudest. Therefore I will leave that at 111 or 127 (whatever is the standard Velocity for the particular song I'm working on), and set the following hits to the next lower value out of my standard velocity list. So for example, if I'm working on an intense Metal track where most of the velocities are at 127, I will leave the first hit of a snare drum Roll at 127, while I reduce the following ones to 111. If I were to start with 111, I'd set the remaining hits to 95, and so forth. Here's how that looks.

Figure 123: Short Snare drum roll with modified velocities

The bars on the bottom of the screen represent the velocities of the hits above. If they are not visible in your DAW, please consult the manual to find out how to turn them on. You can see that the first bar ranges all the way to the top (127), while the remaining three don't go up all the way (111). Make sure to only apply this approach to hits that are part of a sequence. In the case illustrated above, where the standard velocity value is at 127, the next regular Snare drum hit (independent of the pictured drum roll) would be back at 127 again.

If the sequence spans over different drums, I'll start at the standard velocity for every new element of the sequence and adjust any subsequent notes on that same element to the next lower value as described above.

Figure 124: Modified velocities in a sequence spanning different elements of the drum kit

Here are two more examples of really cool fills with velocities changing throughout the patterns. While the standard velocity in these is 127, I use 111 for the first hit on the Toms and the Snare drum, and even go down to 95 for the second hit. This is because they sound really good at high speeds, and in order to hit every drum and move from element to element on the drum kit at a high tempo, drummers will most likely hit softer in the first place.

Figure 125: Softer velocities making a fast part sound more realistic (example 1)

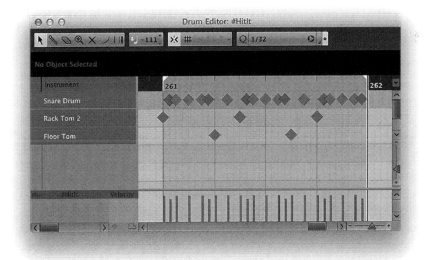

Figure 126: Softer velocities making a fast part sound more realistic (example 2)

In addition to all of the above, I always make sure to emphasize the "on-beat". So if a sequence ends on either count one, two, three, or four, I'll set this particular hit to whatever the standard velocity is as well. Furthermore, if the sequence stretches over more than one beat, I'll check if I need to break it up with an accent on the start of every beat. That doesn't necessarily always have to be the case. Both options, with or without accents on the beat make for a different feel. You'll have to decide which one sounds better on a case-by-case basis.

In the following example, you can see a lower velocity value on the second note of the short 1/8 note Bass drum sequence (consisting of only two directly consecutive notes), and accents on the start of each beat of the Snare drum roll spanning two beats.

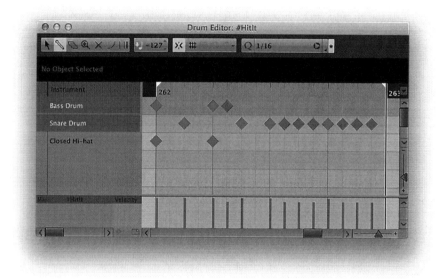

Figure 127: Basic rhythm followed by Snare roll with accents

Ghost notes

As described earlier ghost notes are additional hits complementing the basic Snare drum pattern. They are not as loud as the regular hits. Thus we have to use lower velocity values when programming them. Choose any low velocity value from the standard velocity list (79 and below) and check if the ghost notes still cut through the way you want them to. If they don't use a higher velocity but make sure to keep it lower than the standard velocity of the song. As a rule of thump you can lower the ghost note velocity with the tempo of the song. That's because on a slow ballad a drummer is likely going to hit softer overall. Once the tempo increases he will naturally hit harder and therefore increase the overall volume of the Snare drum hits. Make sure to take that into account when optimizing ghost note velocities but always trust your ears for the final decision.

Hi-hat

The Hi-hat is one of the most crucial elements to get right. It is played throughout all of most songs, and will most likely be hit more often than the Snare or the Bass drum. It is not only hit more often than other elements, but also more consistently. While consistency generally is a good characteristic of a drummer, sounding robotic is not what we want. Yet, this is what we will most likely end up with if we don't work on the velocities.

If you watch real drummers play and listen closely, you will easily spot how they don't hit the Hi-hat with the same intensity every time. The hits on the onbeat, that are played together with the Snare drum or the Bass drum are the loudest, while the others are considerably softer. In terms of programming, they are at the next lower velocity level, maybe even at the next after the next. So, let's say the Hi-hat is played using 1/8 notes throughout a section of a song with a standard velocity of 111. In this scenario, hits would be alternating between 111 and 95, or maybe even 79. This behavior has both stylistic and musical pragmatic properties. For one thing, the groove just breathes more openly when different dynamics are used. Grooves are also easier to play when drummers don't hit with all their energy all the time, especially in fast songs.

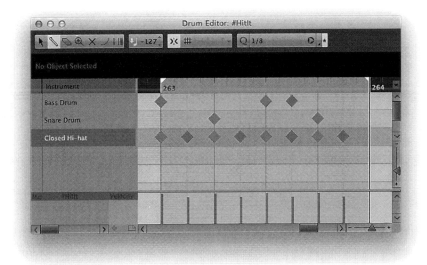

Figure 128: Hi-hat velocities (example 1)

This also applies if there is more than one hit between beats.

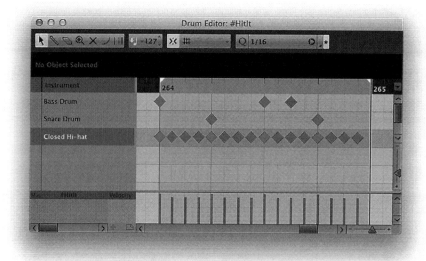

Figure 129: Hi-hat velocities (example 2)

However, there is one exception to that approach and that's when I work on a rather slow, but heavy groove. Due to the lower tempo, it's easier for real drummers to remain consistent, and therefore they will hit with the same amount of power throughout the whole beat. In this example, I used different opening levels on the Hi-hat. I recommend using the more open ones on the on-beats.

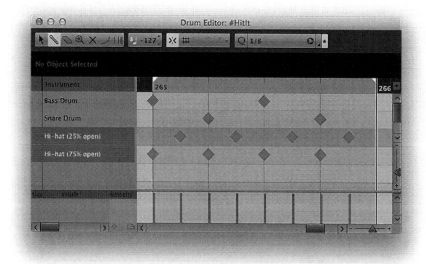

Figure 130: Different Hi-hat opening levels at consistent velocity

Some beats will not be regular four-to-the-floor type of stuff, but more complex grooves with accents on the Snare and/or Bass drum. In this case, accenting the beat according to the click is not the top priority, but rather going with the overall groove.

In the following example, the Bass drum is handled just as you would expect from the above description. The Snare drum is the main element in this beat, and responsible for all the accents that are crucial for this particular groove. Therefore, it is set to 127 all the way through. The slightly opened Hi-hat is the main accompanying element in this beat. The velocities of its hits follow the description from above, with the exception of the hits on beat four in the first and beat three in the second measure. These are set to the next lower velocity value, because they are not accented in this groove. Instead, the fully opened Hi-hat follows along with the accent-providing Snare drum.

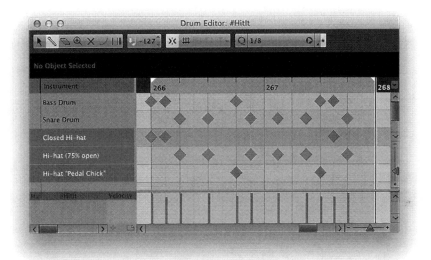

Figure 131: Complex groove with various accents

This technique applies to the Ride cymbal as well, but don't forget that on the Ride cymbal you also have different areas available to hit. So play around with these as well. It's always fun to throw in a Ride bell here and there, too.

Sometimes it even makes sense to add additional hits at a low velocity, even if they wouldn't originally belong there if you just programmed your beat idea straight through, for a more natural feel. The best example for this is if you want to use an open Hi-hat, the Crash cymbal, or the Ride cymbal as an accompanying element. Either one can convey a strong sense of power if played using 1/4 notes. However, sometimes it just doesn't sound quite right for no particular reason. If you come across that problem, try adding additional hits between the original ones, essentially making it an 1/8 note pattern. Just make sure that the additional hits have a considerably lower velocity. In fact, they should be barely audible. In this case they act like ghost notes, but on the accompanying element. You can't really hear them since they are more felt than heard. Yet, they are a great improvement for the beat. Definitely give this technique a try if you ever get stuck and can't seem to get the groove right.

If you go faster, for example, when using 1/8 notes or a very fast tempo, I suggest lowering all the hits by one or two velocity levels. This helps preventing a fake sound in the Crash cymbal and the Ride cymbal. If either is used for the most part of a section of a song, you can add a Crash cymbal at the standard or an accentuated velocity to emphasize chord changes, a new measure, or a new section of the song. Experiment with either, leaving the accompanying element at the reduced velocity for these odd hits, or bringing it up to the same level as the additional Crash cymbal.

Cymbals

When programming drums, cymbals are among the hardest elements to get right. Due to their distinct sound characteristics, it is very difficult to make previously sampled and programmed cymbals not appear fake. I give some tips on how to make cymbals sound more realistic in the bonus chapter on mixing, but these are more of a last resort type of solution, rather than a go-to technique. Therefore, I will highlight how cymbals can be optimized using velocities in the following section.

First of all, there are two different ways of using cymbals. For one thing they can be utilized to emphasize an accent. This occurs at the beginning of a new song section, a new measure, a chord change, or together with an emphasize in the groove of the underlying music of the song. In addition to that they can also be used as an accompanying element (instead of the Hi-hat or Ride cymbal).

The first option is put together rather easily. Use the standard velocity of the song you are working on and see if it sounds good. If you feel it's too weak, bring it up to the next highest velocity. If you are working on a Metal song with a standard velocity of 127 (and therefore can't go any higher), that will almost certainly work for the cymbals as well. However, you can still bring it up a notch by adding a second cymbal on the same hit. Although remember to make sure your virtual drummer's second hand is free, and he's not using it to play any other elements of the drum kit on this particular hit. Also, don't forget to add a kick drum along with the cymbals if you want to emphasize the impact of this hit.

The second option of using the cymbal as an accompanying element is a little trickier. This is due to cymbal sound characteristics. If you hit a cymbal you will initially hear a fair bit of attack, followed by a rather long decay or "sustain" phase. In addition to this already complex behavior, recording cymbals correctly on a live drum set is not an easy task, either. Most of the time you have to take multiple microphones into consideration in order not to run into phasing issues. All of these factors present no problem, as long as you let each cymbal hit in your song ring out to the very end. However, if you want to hit a cymbal again before it has faded out, that's where unnatural sounds occur. You would most likely run into that kind of situation when using a cymbal as an accompanying element, because that is where you would hit it with 1/4 or even 1/8 notes. The simple solution for solving this kind of problem is working with velocities and additional hits, just like we did with the Hi-hat.

The Ride cymbal is an individual case in regards to this problem, since most drum software applications allow you to hit different areas of the cymbal. If you hit the bell, there's usually not much tweaking required. If you hit the edge, everything that's been said about regular cymbals applies.

Crescendos

Crescendos (or build-ups) are sections of a song where one or all elements in the arrangement gradually increase in volume and intensity. We've already touched on this in an earlier chapter, now we'll go into more detail.

You've probably noticed that there are still a lot of velocities in my list that we haven't used yet. We will use some of these for the subtle nuances in Crescendos. First of all, we need to distinguish between different kinds of build-ups. There is one that simply gradually increases volume over time, and one that incorporates additional accents. Lets look at the simple option first.

Most of the time a gradual build-up consists of just the Snare drum, or the Snare drum together with other elements such as the Hi-hat (possibly played with its pedal), the Floor Tom, or the Bass drum. Of course, you don't have to build your Crescendo around the Snare drum. You can do it using any element of the drum kit you like. The principles apply just the same. For now, let's go with a build-up consisting of the Snare drum and the Floor Tom.

First, program a sequence of 1/8 notes using these two elements. Once you've done that, set the first hit in the build-up sequence to one of the lower velocities from the list, for example 31. You can use any value that seems appropriate to you. Just listen to the rest of the music, and make sure the softest hits cut through the arrangement like you want them to. Now, go through all the consecutive hits and gradually increase the velocity with each hit. For the last hit in the sequence, most of the time I will go up to the next higher velocity value than the standard velocity of the song I'm working on. So if the standard velocity of a song is 111, I will program the build-up starting at, let's say 47, and gradually increase the velocity with each hit until I reach 127 on the last hit of the build-up. The next regular hit after the build-up will be at 111 again.

There are two ways to program this kind of Crescendo – linear and exponential. With the first option, the velocities will look somewhat like half of a roof of a house while with the exponential variant they will look like an upwards curve that at first increases slowly and then starts to increase faster. Check out the screenshots below to see what that looks like. Both versions have a different feel. Try both, and use them on different occasions to find the best fit.

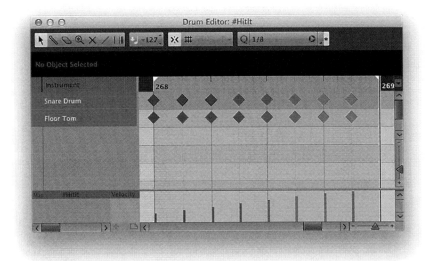

Figure 132: Linear crescendo

Figure 133: Exponential crescendo

Before you start doing this on a regular basis, you should definitely take a look at your MIDI tools. Chances are you will find something similar to a "Line" and a "Curve" tool somewhere. The way these tools work, is that they help you program these build-ups. Select all the hits in a sequence and use either tool to draw the Crescendo over the velocity bars, instead of altering the velocity of every hit by hand.

The second kind of build-up has additional accents build in. So while the velocity still gradually (or exponentially) increases hit after hit in the sequence, every hit that is directly on the beat gets treated differently. First, program the build-up just like you did before, but use 1/16 note Snare drum hits this time for a more outstanding effect. Then take a closer look at the hits directly on the beat. Check the velocity and increase it to the next higher value in our list of velocities. If the initial velocity is very close to the next highest value, you can also use the next value after that. Here's how it looks.

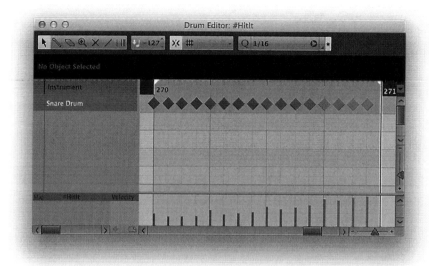

Figure 134: Crescendo with accents

Double Bass drum beats

When you deal with double Bass drum beats, most of the time you will probably be working on a Metal song. As we've discussed earlier, Metal productions are often heavily edited after they've been recorded. Especially the original Bass and Snare drum, recordings are often "triggered" for a consistent sound. Subsequently, the original hits are replaced with one or more samples. The reason behind this, is that drummers sometimes will have a hard time hitting really hard when playing so fast. Consequently, they will hit softer and the sound will not be as fierce as desired. For us, this is good news because less tweaking is required. In fact, in modern Metal I aim for very little velocity variation in double Bass passages. Depending on the quality and the sound of the samples of the drum software I'm using, I will choose a velocity that sounds heavy enough, usually 111 or 95. You can do this independently of the actual volume of the velocity of your choice. If you like it, use it. If it's not loud enough, but its sound characteristic is still what you are after, just turn up the respective fader in your drum software's mixer. I start off the double bass passage with the standard velocity of the song and use the velocity I've just chosen as described above for the rest.

Blast beats

We've touched on Blast beats as the most extreme grooves out there in the Metal chapter. We've established that they sometimes come close to a machine-like sound because of their precision and sheer brutality. While we definitely want precision and brutality, we don't want "robotic" playback. That's why we need to pay special attention to velocities on Blast beats.

Similar to the double Bass grooves, Blast beats are very fast and drummers will have a hard time hitting hard throughout the whole performance. However, with Blast beats, recordings are mostly not so heavily triggered so that they don't sound robotic as mentioned above. This depends on the type of Blast beat though. For example, a traditional Blast can still be played hitting hard at fairly high tempos, whereas a Hammer Blast or a Gravity Blast would be nearly impossible to maintain with good consistency at high tempos. In this section we'll cover the types of Blast beats that need special attention, and we can discuss how to optimize them. Those that are not mentioned can be programmed using the same principles as all other beats.

The Hammer Blast consists of the Bass drum, the Snare drum, and the Hi-hat (or the Ride/Crash cymbals) all being hit at the same time. You can probably imagine how hard it would be to hit all these elements with the same intensity over an extended period of time. Therefore, I will program all the hits in a Hammer Blast pattern one or two velocity steps lower than the standard velocity of the song.

With the Gravity Blast, the Snare drum is constantly playing 1/16 notes at a very fast tempo. The way real drummers handle this is by not actually hitting the drum for every note. Instead they let the stick bounce back up from the drum skin to save energy. As a result the Snare drum is not very loud in Gravity Blasts. I usually go for a velocity of 111 or 95 here. For the Bass drum and the Hi-hat, I use the approach from above.

The Skank beat is pretty straightforward, but at high tempos it's important to lower the velocity of every second hit on the accompanying element for a realistic feel. I usually go one or two steps down from the standard velocity of the song.

Fine-tuning velocities

Now that you've gone through all that you are probably thinking that even with velocities adjusted all the hits are still static and predictable to a certain degree. That depends on your drum software, though. Good software has multiple samples of each element of the kit at the same velocity. So, let's say you program two consecutive hits at the same velocity. If you use good drum software, you won't hear the same sound twice and there will be a difference in the sound even if the velocity is the same.

However, there is a way to take this even further. Most recording software applications will aid you in the process. Take a look at your DAW's MIDI options and settings. Look out for something along the lines of "Random", "Randomization", or "Random Velocity". This setting will allow you to define how far off from the programmed velocity any hit can actually play back. Ideally, your recording software has "+" and "-" parameters for this. So for example, a hit that's been programmed at a velocity of 100 with the Random parameters set to +/- 5 will actually play back at a random velocity anywhere from 95 to 105. This will give you a good variance in the velocities and make for a natural sound.

> *Note that if you program hits at 127 with the random parameters set to, let's say, +/-10, this is not going to give you hits at 137. 127 is still as loud as it gets. So you will most likely end up with a lot of hits at 127 and some hits between 117 and 127. If you are working at 127 to begin with, you are going to be just fine though, since you are most likely looking for a heavy feel anyway, and the variation in your drum software that I described above will do the rest.*

If you don't have the +/- parameters but a more generalized control set instead, the best way of finding out how it affects the sound is turning it up all the way to hear an obvious effect and then turn it back down slowly until it sounds natural. Don't pay too much attention to any numbers or meters that might be related to the parameters. Trust your ears.

If your DAW doesn't have these settings at all, you are left to your own devices in this situation. However, it's less work than you might think. After you've finished programming your drums, use your recording software's pencil tool to go in and alter every hit just ever so slightly by hand. Personally, I hardly ever go over +/-7, but once again this is entirely up to you and your DAW, what kind of sound and feel you are going for, and what sounds right to you.

Bonus chapter: Odd time signatures

Contrary to popular belief, not all music is written in 4/4 time. It might be the way to go for most stuff on the radio, but there is a whole other world beyond the limitations of four beats in one measure. Granted, odd time signatures are mostly used by more exotic genres, but there is still some use for them in popular music as well. Therefore, it seems appropriate to at least broach the subject. We are going to discuss three odd time signatures in this bonus chapter to give you an idea of their challenges and possibilities. Don't think these are the only ones out there though. Naturally, the number of odd time signatures possible is somewhat endless. We will start with 6/8 time and work our way to 5/4 and 7/4.

6/8 time

As 6/8 time is an even time signature (there are six beats in each measure), we can utilize a similar rule of thumb to build our grooves as in 4/4 time. We can either start with the Snare drum on beats three and six, or on beat four only. The Bass drum could than go on beats one and four, or just on beat one respectively.

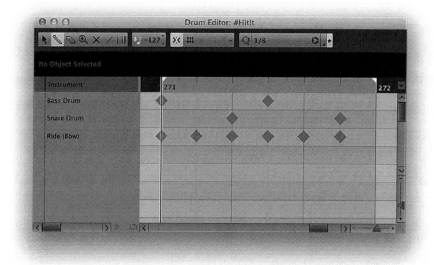

Figure 135: 6/8 time starting point (example 1)

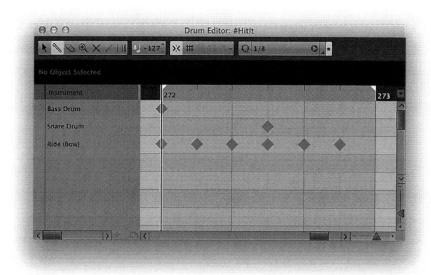

Figure 136: 6/8 time starting point (example 2)

If you listen to these grooves on their own they might sound a little weird, maybe even uncomfortable. That's because we are so used to hearing 4/4 time on the radio all the time. Try listening to them for a few measures on repeat and you will get accustomed to them quickly. If you already have same music in 6/8 time to go along with them, you can start customizing these grooves right away.

Since this time signature is often used in a slower, ballad types of songs, it's probably a good idea to add a few Bass drum hits or some Snare drum ghost notes here and there to mix it up a little. As we've said, you don't have to stick to these guidelines. They just serve to give you a starting point.

Here are some excerpts from grooves of popular songs in 6/8 time. Can you name them? This first one is from a Pop song with a very powerful female singer.

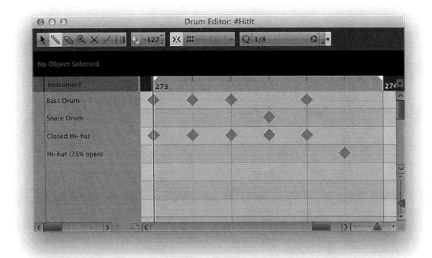

Figure 137: Popular 6/8 example 1, Tempo: 64 BPM

This next groove is used by a Metal band on one of the singles on their breakthrough album, but it is also used by one of history's most influential rock bands on one of their greatest hits.

Figure 138: Popular 6/8 example 2, Tempo: 48 BPM (Metal) / 64 BPM (Rock)

Here is a fill that belongs to the aforementioned Metal band's song that might help you identify it.

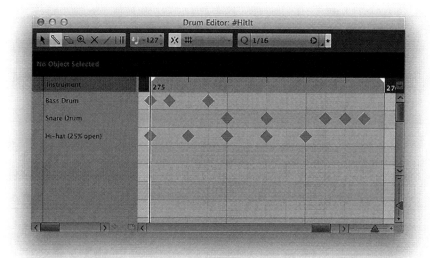

Figure 139: Popular 6/8 fill example, Tempo: 48 BPM

Last but not least, here is something heavier from a more recent British Metal band. This is used in the chorus of one of their singles.

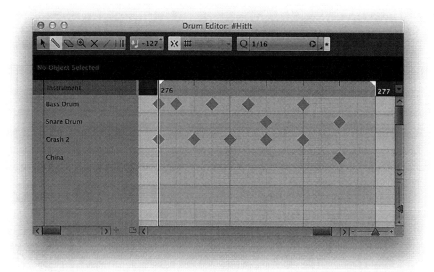

Figure 140: Popular 6/8 example 3, Tempo: 190 BPM

Happy guessing!

The next odd time signature we will discuss is 5/4 time.

5/4 time

In 4/4 time we used a simple rule to build our beats, the Bass drum goes on beats one and three, while the Snare drum goes on beats two and four. This provides us with a great starting point. In 5/4 time, we can't make these general statements anymore. At first this may seem like a difficulty, but if we look closer it's more of an advantage. We are totally free to put our Bass and Snare drum hits wherever we think they might fit. As a matter of fact, we are free to do that in any time signature, but this is more relevant in odd time signatures.

When working with odd time signatures, most of the time the underlying music will have a very distinct groove. So, the logical way to write drum tracks for it is simple: lock-in with the music just like we did in 4/4 time.

At first, spread your Bass and Snare drum hits somewhat evenly across the measure. You can start with the Snare drum on beats two and five, or if you're headed for a half-time feel, try putting it on the off-beat of beat three. Fill up the measure with Bass drum hits as you see fit. This could be 1/16 notes double bass hits all the way through if you are working on a Metal track, or just 1/4 or 1/8 notes here and there in a Pop or Rock setting.

Once you've set that up start listening to the rest of the music in your song. Most of the time when a song happens to be in an odd time signature, there is a pretty obvious reason for it like a very distinct rhythm on some of the guitar or vocal riffs that involves a lot of accents. Try listening for those and program your drum tracks accordingly. If you can, lock-in with the rest of the music just like I explained above. This is particularly easy in odd time signatures if the guitar track of the song involves a lot of palm muting.

Another thing that you can try to do is to vary your accompanying element. So, if you were to use the Ride cymbal going along to your Bass and Snare drum in 1/4 notes, try adding two 1/8 notes for one of the 1/4 notes in your beat. This seems to work quite well before or after the Snare drum hits, but feel free to experiment with other positions within your groove as well.

Once again this whole field of 5/4 beats is something that calls for a very customized approach. Nevertheless here are a few examples to give you an idea of how beats in that time signature can sound.

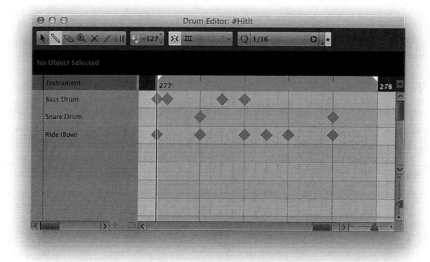

Figure 141: Grid 1/16 notes, Appropriate tempo: 90-150 BPM

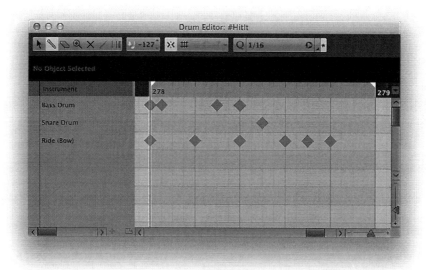

Figure 142: Grid 1/16 notes, Appropriate tempo: 90-150 BPM

Depending on the tempo of your song the following beats might be better suited for Metal applications.

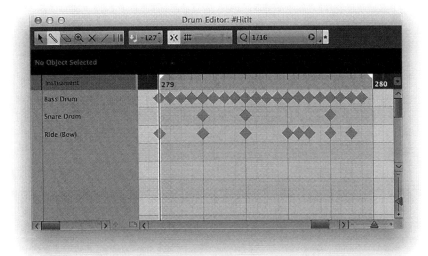

Figure 143: Grid 1/16 notes, Appropriate tempo: 90-180 BPM

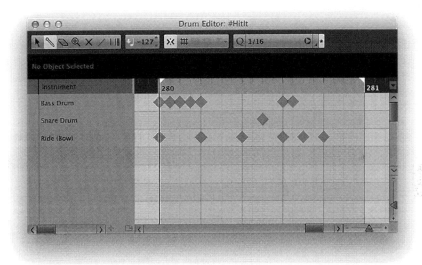

Figure 144: Grid 1/16 notes, Appropriate tempo: 120-180 BPM

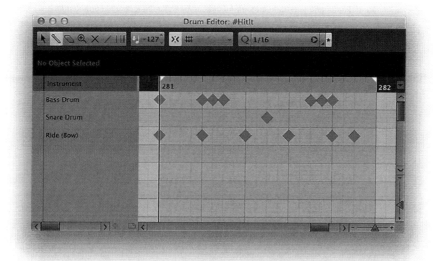

Figure 145: Grid 1/16 notes, Appropriate tempo: 100-220 BPM

Now that we've got an idea of what's going on in 5/4, let's move on to 7/4.

7/4 time

Basically everything that's been said about 5/4 time applies to 7/4 time as well with the only difference that we now have to fill seven beats instead of five in every measure. I highly encourage listening to your song and find a beat that fits it. If you need starting points, try the Snare drum on beats three and seven or the off-beat of beat six for a regular feel, and on beat five for a half-time kind of feel. Add the Bass drum around the measure as you see fit. Here are some examples to get you started, but again, try to come up with your own customized ideas wherever possible.

This example is kind of percussive because of the Hi-hat barking. If you don't like that, you can exchange it for a more straight Hi-hat or Ride (or even Crash cymbal) pattern.

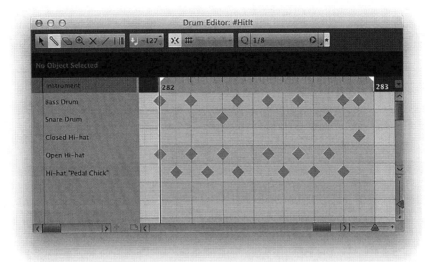

Figure 146: Grid 1/8 notes, Appropriate tempo: 120-200 BPM

This next groove comes straight out of one of my own songs.

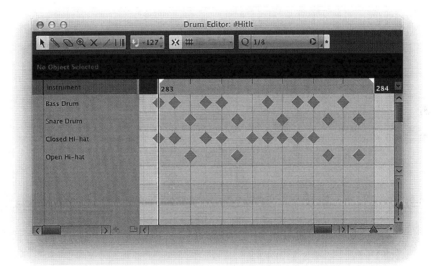

Figure 147: Grid 1/8 notes, Appropriate tempo: 95-175 BPM

Here are three more ideas covering both regular and somewhat half-time feel.

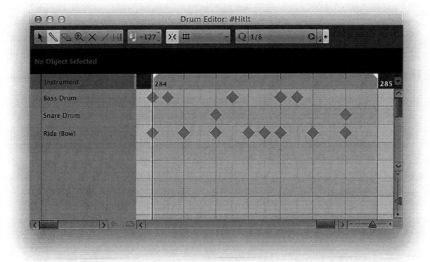

Figure 148: Grid 1/8 notes, Appropriate tempo: 95-200 BPM

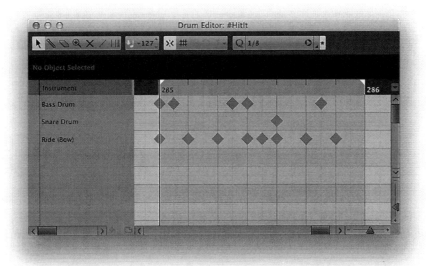

Figure 149: Grid 1/8 notes, Appropriate tempo: 95-200 BPM

Figure 150: Grid 1/16 notes, Appropriate tempo: 130-200 BPM

To close this chapter, here are two more beats for the Metal crowd.

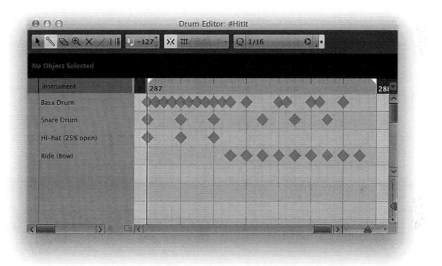

Figure 151: Grid 1/16 notes, Appropriate tempo: 100-180 BPM

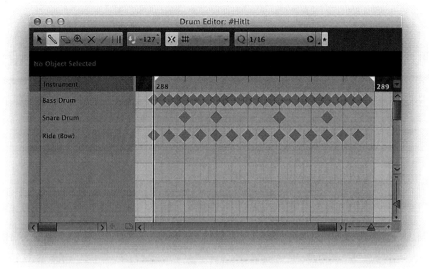

Figure 152: Grid 1/16 notes, Appropriate tempo: 80-200 BPM

Bonus chapter: Mixing tips

Programmed drums offer a lot of convenience. You don't have to bother with setting up a real drum kit, place all the microphones as best as possible, and record for several hours if not days, let alone the mighty cost of a professional studio. For some musicians, producers and songwriters, programmed drums might even be the only way of getting drums on their tracks because they don't have access to a real drummer or the necessary equipment and rooms. While these advantages certainly speak for the use of programmed drums, there will always be critics that argue that programmed drums never sound like the real thing – no matter how much you work on velocities and quantization settings. Sometimes though, the nay-sayers can be convinced if extra effort has been put into the mixing process.

Mixing drums is a complex task. It's certainly not something a beginner can achieve at a professional level right from the beginning. Moreover, different pieces of drum software differ greatly in terms of sound quality and mixing flexibility. The following tips and tricks should help you to improve your drum sound. For anyone wishing to dig deeper in the topic of mixing, and not only drums but all the other elements of a modern music arrangement, I highly recommend "The Systematic Mixing Guide" by Australian Engineer and Producer *Ermin "Ermz" Hamidovic*. Definitely check it out if you want to take the next step towards becoming a professional mixer.

Different types of Drum Software and Routing

Before we can talk about the details of mixing, we have to establish a few technical parameters. First of all there are basically two kinds of drum software applications out there. On one hand there are products that offer ready-made sounds that will most likely fit into the kind of context they were created for. There are special drum kits (and/or expansion packs) for Pop, Rock, and Metal, as well as for a whole lot of other applications as well. On the other hand, there are "neutral" products that simply deliver professionally recorded and unprocessed sounds that leave the user with the option to process them according to their needs. If you are using the later, you will most likely have to look into advanced mixing techniques.

The first group is a little more limited, but it can still be tailored to fit individual needs better than right out of the box. These products were made with the intention in mind to provide the user with something useful right away, as opposed to them having to come up with a professional mix all by themselves. Therefore, the manufacturers hired a producer that would create professional mix-ready presets for you to use. Usually you have to insert an instance of the drum software on a MIDI track in your recording software and you are left with a stereo signal of the whole drum set. You can use that to alter the overall volume of the drums or apply customized equalizer settings to further shape the sound. As you may have noticed, this is not very flexible. In order to be able to use the full capabilities of your DAW, we need to route all the signals of the drum kit (Bass drum, Snare drum, Toms, Cymbals and so forth) to individual tracks in our recording software. Look for an option within your drum software that's called "Multi Outs", "Multiple Outputs", "Multichannel", or similar and activate it. Please refer to your drum software's manual to find the exact setting. You should now see individual channels for each piece of the drum kit in your DAW.

Please note: some drum software products might also offer you a mixer inside the software that allows you to tweak the sounds with integrated Faders and

> *Plug-ins. Feel free to use them instead of routing all the different signals out to your recording software. If the quality of the integrated plug-in is good, you can achieve similar results with less effort.*

As I've mentioned earlier, the more ready-made drum software products have been pre-mixed to fit certain applications. This usually involves different types of dynamic processing that cannot be undone. In order to avoid ending up with an over-compressed sound, I don't recommend using additional compression on these types of products. However, it's totally fine to use extra equalizer adjustments to shape the sound. We will now briefly go over each piece of the drum kit and discuss how different equalizer settings affect the sound.

Cymbals

A typical sound check at a live show usually starts with the Bass drum. In this case I'd like to go ahead with the cymbals though because they are oftentimes the first elements that give away whether any particular drum track is real or programmed.

So how do you prevent that from happening? The answer is simpler than you might think. Lower the volume of the cymbal. That's all. If you lower the cymbals by 3 dB to 6 dB they will be way less noticeable and therefore harder to make out as real or fake.

Another way to "hide" your programmed cymbals is by applying what's called a Low-Pass filter. Essentially, this means turning down all the high frequencies of the cymbals down to a certain point. Try going lower with your frequency setting until the cymbals sound unnatural to you. At this point go back up just a little bit and leave it there. You should now have successfully removed some overtones that might be responsible for your cymbals fake sound.

> *Note: that this is somewhat counterintuitive to what you would most likely do to a mix with real drums. Therefore it's not necessarily going to make your cym-*

> *bals sound better, but they will probably blend in better with the rest of the music, stand out less and therefore will be less noticeable as being programmed.*

Speaking about counterintuitive things to do: if your drum software has some sort of "bleed" control, you can try and deactivate that. What this will do is let other elements of the drum kit bleed into the Cymbal, or so-called "overhead" microphones. This further distracts from the actual cymbals themselves. While you would normally most likely cut out all the low frequencies in the cymbal microphones as well, you can try leaving them in for the sake of a more natural sound.

Bass drum

The Bass drum needs special attention, as it is very important that its sound fits the genre of the song. From Pop to Rock, or even to Metal, it gradually gets more intense and "in your face". For a Pop sound, try cutting out some of the high and high-mid frequencies.

A Rock Bass drum usually has a little more presence, so maybe boost a little in the area between 2k and 8k Hz. If it sounds too "woody", cut out some low-mid frequencies between 250 and 500 Hz. Don't worry, if it sounds woody you'll know, even if that description may sound strange right now. Last but not least, you can try boosting a few dB around 60-100 Hz for a little more low end.

Metal has by far the most prominent Bass drum sounds. If it hasn't been done already on whatever preset you are using, heavily boost the 2k-8k area to get a good, "clicky" sound, cut out the low-mid frequencies and boost the lows accordingly. Remember to check the Bass drum in comparison to the Bass guitar as well.

Snare drum

The most important thing with Snare drums is choosing the right sound to begin with. There are a lot of different Snare drums and they all sound different.

So before you even start thinking about equalization, make sure to choose the right sample for your taste and needs within your drum software.

Once you have settled on the sample you want to use, it's safe to say you can cut out all the low frequencies up to 80 or 100 Hz on most Snare drums. Other than that, it really depends a lot on the specific Snare drum sample that you are using. If you boost the area around 250 Hz, it usually gives the sound a little more body. Whether or not you have to boost and/or cut any of the low-mid, high-mid, and high frequencies really depends on the sample you are using.

One general technique you can use is boosting any of the three equalizer bands just mentioned and then sweep through their whole respective frequency range. That way, you can identify frequencies that sound particularly good or bad. If you find a bad sounding frequency, just turn it down to any negative dB amount that is necessary to remove the unwanted sound. If you come across a good sounding frequency, just turn the extreme boost down to a more moderate level.

If you are dealing with an extra Snare bottom microphone that is pointed right at the Snare wires that one usually covers a lot of high frequencies. It's safe to say you can cut out a good amount of low end on this one. Also try flipping the phase on the Snare bottom microphone and check if it sounds better or worse that way, together with the Snare top microphone. Usually, if you use a pre-mixed drum set, this will have been done already and you don't have to do it anymore. As a matter of fact, in this case, it will worsen your sound. But if you don't use a preset or an advanced drum software that requires you to mix the drum set all by yourself, you definitely have to do that.

Toms

Toms are probably the most popular and generally usable components of any drum software. While there are most likely always people who don't like the Bass drums, Snare drums, or Cymbals that come with any particular drum software, the Toms seem to be appreciated most of the time. Therefore they need less equalization than other elements of the drum kit. If you do find yourself in the need to customize any given Tom sounds, they can be approached much like the Bass drum. You will find low frequencies between 60 and 120 Hz, "woody" and a certain kind of "boxyness" between 250 and 500 Hz, and a good amount of attack in the area between 2k and 8k Hz. Boost and/or cut as desired.

Note: these are just rough frequency ranges that will differ between different Tom models and shell sizes. They should give you a good starting point, though. In addition to that, you can always use the sweeping technique described above to find frequencies to boost and cut.

Room sound and Reverb

If your drums already sound good you are at a great starting point. Adding some Reverb might help them to sound even bigger. When it comes to Reverb there are a number of different options. I like 'Plate' type reverbs for the Snare drum and the Toms. 'Hall' reverbs are nice if you need a really big sound. They can also be useful in adding depth to your cymbals. Last but not least, 'Room' reverbs can make for a really natural sound that, if dialed in properly, can give you the feeling as if you were standing right next to the drum kit. Professional mixers often combine these different types of reverbs to get their desired sound.

Don't overdue it with reverb on the Bass drum and the lower Toms, or else the overall sound will get muddy and undefined because the low frequencies tend to cause a rumbling build-up, especially with long reverb times. Either add less reverb to these elements or cut the lower frequencies on the reverb.

If you find yourself with insufficient or unnatural sounding drums, you can get them to sound a little more distant by turning up the room microphones (in case your drum software offers any) and/or by adding more reverb as you normally would to either the drums as a whole or to certain elements of the drum kit (like the Toms or the Snare drum). By doing that, you might be able to hide them away from listeners' attention, and thereby distract them from weak samples.

That may not be the ideal way to mix your drums but it can get you out of a tricky situation from time to time.

Parallel compression

This is a technique primarily used in Metal as it makes drums sound extra-heavy. In the beginning of this chapter I recommended not adding any more compression to pre-processed samples. Parallel compression is an exception to this rule, as the drum samples aren't really compressed themselves. Instead a compressed version of them is added. The way to achieve this technically is by routing all the different tracks from your drum software to your DAW individually (see Multichannel routing described above). Then create an FX channel inside your DAW and put your favorite compressor plug-in on the track. Use the lowest Attack and the highest Ratio setting possible. Now turn down the fader of this track all the way. Use the FX sends of each individual drum channel to send a fair amount of signal to said FX track. Start playback and slowly bring up the fader of the FX track while listening closely. You should hear your drums sounding considerably punchier.

If you don't hear the effect right away try a drastic A/B-comparison. Turn up the FX channel all the way (or maybe even above 0 dB if it doesn't clip at that point) and mute/unmute it while playing back your track. It should be pretty obvious now how parallel compression affects the sound and you can make adjustments from there by experimenting with some parameters. You can send more or less signal from the drums to the FX channel. It doesn't have to be the same amount for every drum. Trust your ears. Watch out for the Cymbals. If they stand out too much you can completely omit parallel compression on them (Just turn of the FX send on their channels) or you can use a low-pass filter on the FX track to preserve the additional punch but get rid of some nasty overtones at the same time.

Sample replacement

If you turn up the radio chances are you are not hearing the drums the artist recorded in the studio. The reason for that is that a lot of mixing engineers use sample replacement to enhance the sound of the drums. Thereby they will take the original recording and use sample replacement software to achieve a specific sound. As you can imagine this opens up literally endless possibilities. You can mix in just a tiny amount of a certain sample to add some specific flavor to the sound. Or you can add more than one sample to form a complex stack of different sounds. Whether you choose to just add in additional sounds to the original recording or to replace it completely is up to you. Sometimes, when the original recording of a live drum set is very bad, mixing engineers use the latter method as a last resort in order to save a project.

You can either record your own samples or you can use commercially available sample packs. Quality and prices differ so make sure to listen to sound examples before you make your purchase. There is also a vast array of free samples available on various forums on the Internet. If you get sample replacement software it will most likely come with a library of professionally recorded samples as well.

If you get the chance to try out sample replacement software definitely give it a shot. You will need to set up your drum software for multichannel routing as described above in order to apply sample replacement.

Final words

Congratulations! If you've made it this far and applied some of the principles I've laid out in this book I'm very confident that you are now able to program realistic sounding professional drum tracks. I strongly believe that this skill will take your songs to the next level and boost your career a great deal. The music business certainly isn't an easy one to be in but if you succeed by doing what you love it's all the more rewarding. Good luck for the challenges that lie ahead of you.

If you've liked this book it would mean the world to me if you told your friends about it. Leave a comment on my website or on my Facebook page or send a tweet. Sign up to my e-mail list and make sure to join the #HitIt Facebook group to get in touch with other producers all over the world and for an exchange of experiences.

Website: www.drumprogrammingguide.com
E-mail list: www.drumprogrammingguide.com/readers-newsletter
Facebook page: www.drumprogrammingguide.com/facebook-page
Facebook group: www.drumprogrammingguide.com/facebook-group
Twitter: www.drumprogrammingguide.com/twitter

Thank you so much for supporting me by buying this book!

#HitIt

Made in the USA
San Bernardino, CA
30 December 2015